"Race" and the "Civilizing Mission"

"RACE"
AND THE
"CIVILIZING MISSION"

Their Implications for the Framing of
Blackness and African Personhood,
1800-1960

An Inaugural Presentation
- *by* -
Waibinte Elekima Wariboko

Africa World Press, Inc.

P.O. Box 1892

Trenton, NJ 08607

P.O. Box 48

Asmara, ERITREA

Africa World Press, Inc.

P.O. Box 1892

Trenton, NJ 08607

P.O. Box 48

Asmara, ERITREA

Book and Cover design: Saverance Publishing Services

Library of Congress Cataloging-in-Publication Data

Wariboko, Waibinte E. (Waibinte Elekima), 1956-
  "Race" and the "civilizing mission" : their implications for the framing of Blackness and African personhood, 1800-1960 / Waibinte Elekima Wariboko.
  p. cm.
  Includes bibliographical references.
  ISBN 1-59221-769-9 (hardcover) -- ISBN 1-59221-770-2 (pbk.)
  1. Race--Religious aspects--Christianity. 2. Missions--Africa. 3. Christianity--Africa. 4. Identity (Psychology)--Religious aspects--Christianity. 5. Personalism. I. Title.
  BT734.W37 2010
  266.00967'09034--dc22
                              2010025033

TABLE OF CONTENTS

PREFATORY COMMENTS

The publication format, on the suggestion of the publisher, has parted with one standard conventional practice: in addition to the expanded version of the inaugural address, readers will have the benefit of appreciating how two colleagues have received and reacted to the issues raised in the address. As the author of the inaugural address, I perceive immense advantages in this venture; and I wish to express my profound gratitude to the publisher, Mr. Kassahun Checole, for "thinking outside of the box."

Broadly speaking both the inaugural address as well as the review essays have been informed by the anti-colonial and/or postcolonial intellectual worldviews. Given these worldviews, in one way or another, these essays are intended to destabilize the dominant discourses of imperial Europe about Africa during the period under review. As postcolonial critiques, these essays in varying degrees have emphasized one central point: the practice of "naming" prevalent in colonial discourses—history, philosophy, pure and applied sciences, social sciences, linguistics, and literature, for example—are not "innocent"; they are instead ideologically constructed and driven to select and to legitimate the selection of certain parts of the world (in this case Africa) for European domination and exploitation.

Divided into four mutually related and reinforcing parts, the address starts off with a discussion on the notions of "race" and the "civilizing mission." Both concepts, drawing inspiration from the works of Paul Gilroy, Kwame A. Appiah, Phillip D. Curtin, and Charles W. Mills, among others, are perceived as dialectically related social products that can be apprehended and chronologically mapped in detail. "Race," as discussed and argued throughout, engendered the "civilizing mission" as an instrument for achieving its objectives in the African continent; and, in a mutually reinforcing manner, they worked in unison to vilify "blackness" and African personhood in order to valorize "whiteness" during the period leading up to colonialism and after.

Since this wanton exercise of demonizing "blackness" was ideologically driven and designed to justify the conquest, subjugation and colonization of Africa, including the crude and unrestrained exploitation of its natural resources and its inhabitants who were considered not fully human, the efforts to decolonize the continent began with a frantic search for a new identity and personhood. That search ultimately led to the inauguration of an Africa-centered resistance narrative called the "Historiography of Self-Assertion." Through a critique of the "Historiography of Self-Assertion" and the Eurocentric imperial narratives that framed "blackness" pejoratively, the ideological factors that were at work in the cultural politics of knowledge production about Africa, including their implications for the uses and/or abuses of anthropological, ethnographic, historical and socio-linguistic "evidence," were discussed and analyzed. Finally, in chronicling and mapping these ideological tensions between "whiteness" and "blackness" over time, the inaugural address fully explored the theoretical character of individual and national identity construction.

The response-essays, which are set out in the second section of this publication, are intended to provide additional comments and insights on the issues addressed above. These response-essays, in doing this, have not only highlighted the strengths and weaknesses of the arguments in the original address presented in section one, but they have also brought critical and refreshing perspectives to bear on the unending dialogue generated by the themes discussed in that address. Here is the ultimate benefit of the publisher's suggestion and advice: the enrichment of scholarship through the inaugural address and the structured review and/or response-essays from colleagues outside of the host university—the Mona Campus of the University of the West Indies in Jamaica.

In "Race, Slavery and Imperialism: Knowledge Production and Personhood," Bersselaar has argued that how the imperialist discourse on blackness was consumed was dependent in part on local and individual circumstances. He therefore makes a distinction between imperial propaganda in the metropolis and the development of local traditions of imperial knowledge and propaganda. The Igbo-speaking people, he reminded us, had associated with the hamitic hypothesis with a view to enhancing their personhood locally- that is within southern Nigeria. This is refreshing because, from the standpoint of the address, the hamitic hypothesis diminished African personhood without exceptions and qualifications.

In "Christian Missionaries, Racism and the Emergence of an African Historiography of 'Self-Damnation,'" Njoku severely critiqued the "pro-alienation discourse" that has in part informed the "Historiography of Self-Assertion." The "Historiography of Self-Assertion," which was promoted by the nationalist historians of Africa, was very highly condemnatory of Africa's postcolonial elites because they were considered "alienated" from the peoples they sought to govern. However, after reexamining some of the theories underpinning the "pro-alienation discourse," Njoku concluded thus: "There is no convincing historical/empirical evidence to support the claim to severance of ties between the elite and their various local communities." The evidence reveals, Njoku further contended: "that the notion of an alienated elite was [wrongly] premised on an attempt to hold these people squarely responsible for African postcolonial problems."

These review-essays and the inaugural address collectively reinforce one point: the narratives we construct as scholars will always invariable depend on our intellectual world view.

THE EXPANDED INAUGURAL ADDRESS

"RACE"

AND THE

"CIVILIZING MISSION"

THEIR IMPLICATIONS FOR THE FRAMING OF BLACKNESS AND AFRICAN PERSONHOOD, 1800-1960

- WAIBINTE E. WARIBOKO -

Introduction

The Pro Vice Chancellor and Principal, Professor Gordon Shirley, the Campus Registrar, Dr. Camille Bell-Hutchinson, the Deans of Faculties present, and the Dean of the Faculty of Humanities and Education in particular, Dr. Swithin Wilmot, colleagues and students from the Department of History and Archaeology, other distinguished friends and well wishers from within and outside of the Mona Campus of the University of the West Indies, I wish to thank you very heartily for honoring the invitation to this memorable and auspicious inaugural professorial address.

It is customary and appropriate, on this special occasion, to recognize and salute those persons responsible for putting in place the cultural facilities and roadmaps that helped to shape and inform my search for self-realization from childhood to adulthood: mum and dad, the late Mrs. Elizabeth E.W. Briggs and Chief Elekima W. Briggs. I hereby record my immense and profound indebtedness to all of those teachers, in particular Professors Robin Horton, Ebiegberi Joseph Alagoa, and Tom MacCaskie, who guided me at various times through the different stages of the formal school system in Nigeria and England before I joined the Mona Campus of the University of the West Indies in Jamaica as an employee.

On the Mona Campus I have also benefited immensely from the genuine and amiable advice of many persons and colleagues, in particular Professor Aggrey Brown, the former Dean of the Faculty of Humanities and Education, Professor Emeritus Roy Augier, Professor Brian Moore (now at the Colgate University in the United States), Dr. Swithin Wilmot, and my dear sweetheart, Dr. Cynthia Onyefulu. "An unwoven basket," so goes a Kalabari-Ijo proverb, "cannot carry refuse." You have all helped and contributed, in one way or another, to the advancement of my professional career and social welfare since I joined the Mona Campus academic community in 1993.

In this inaugural address I intend to discuss some of the ideological issues revolving around "race" and the "civilizing mission" that had informed and influenced the uses and/or abuses of "evidence" in the construction of African personhood and blackness between 1800 and 1960. I have chosen to discuss this subject for one principal reason. Having dealt with the ideological constructs and/or fictions of "race" and the "civilizing mission" in nearly all scholarly outputs leading up to this address, I now wish to more fully explore and reflect, with this august audience, their implications for the construction of African personhood and blackness. Highlighting these ideological issues in knowledge production generally, and how they could influence the uses and/or abuses of "evidence" in particular, directly begs for one of the age-old questions in ethnographic, anthropological, philosophical, and historical research: What is evidence? Evidence could be perceived and defined in several ways; but, for the purposes and aims of this lecture, I have chosen to adopt the following definition offered by Lewis R. Gordon.

> Evidence is paradoxically that which has been hidden but revealed as a conduit for the appearance of another hidden reality. In effect, then, it is an appearance that enables appearance, but it is an appearance that requires thinking in order to appear. *In short, it is not an appearance that stimulates thought but a form of thought that stimulates appearance.* This means that evidence is always symbolic; it always refers beyond itself. Because whether affirmed or rejected, it always extends itself publicly for assessment, *evidence is peculiarly social.* And since it is social, evidence is subject to the complex exchange of inter-subjective activities. Evidence must, in other words, be subject to "norms" and "criteria."[1] [My emphasis]

Since "evidence is peculiarly social" and also "subject to the complex exchange of inter-subjective activities," among other characteristics highlighted above, it lends itself to cultural interrogation from one historical epoch to another. Bearing these characteristics in mind, I intend to discuss how "evidence" was subjected to the "norms" and "criteria" jointly fashioned and put in place by the philosophers and agents of "race" and the "civilizing mission" interested in the universal enthronement of whiteness over blackness between 1800 and 1960- the decade of Africa's independence from European colonialism. The philosophers and agents referred to, perceiving themselves as the bearers of light and reason and the producers of useable political knowledge for European domination of the world, undertook to theorize and explain the African social and cultural universe through the lenses of white normativity.

Chronicling and reinterpreting the enthronement of whiteness over blackness could provide yet another window of fresh opportunity to re-problematize the relevance of history as an invaluable resource for understanding some of the current concepts underpinning global identity politics. Explicitly or implicitly, because this exploration of the past is being aimed at illuminating contemporary and current global issues of sociopolitical and cultural interest, it will also be reinforcing the epistemological relevance of anti-Cartesian views—that is, those views opposed to the position of Descartes regarding the overall value of history to society. The latter had, for example, argued that:

> [T]hose who travel too long end by being strangers in their own homes and those who study curiously the actions of antiquity are ignorant of what is done among ourselves today …, and men who try to model their own acts upon them are prone to the madness of romantic paladins and mediate hyperbolical deeds.[2]

To know the past, as all anti-Cartesians have argued, one must be very firmly rooted in the present; and knowledge of the past, far from keeping one ignorant of what goes on among us today, actually enhances an understanding of the present and the future. According to that great North African philosopher, St. Augustine: the theme of change and continuity, as reflected and represented in the relationship between the past, the present, and the future, could also be described as "'the present of things past, the present of things present, and the present of things future.'"[3]

The epistemological significance of the points articulated by anti-Cartesians and St. Augustine was not lost on the intellectuals of African descent. Drawn from the mother continent and the New World African diaspora, they produced *a politically usable past* to ideologically validate, inform, facilitate and encourage the decolonization of the continent; and they also simultaneously worked assiduously to reconstruct the battered image of blackness and African personhood. These intellectuals, adopting the Gramscian perspective, included all those (scholars, statesmen and stateswomen, publicists and activists) who were able to create for Africa "a coherent and reasoned account of [its place in] the world"[4] that challenged the mystifications of Eurocentric and colonial historiographies informed and legitimated by the ideologies of "race" and the "civilizing mission." For very obvious reasons these intellectuals realized that, in order to change the existing African consciousness, they had to first challenge, refute and rewrite those historical race-oriented narratives that had shaped and informed the African self-knowledge since the imposition of the civilizing mission and colonialism on the continent.

However, with the attainment of self-governance and the continent's regrettable inability to overcome its nagging and painful socioeconomic problems, that body of spirited and nationalistic intellectual endeavor that had facilitated decolonization, which became known as "The New African Historiography" or "The Historiography of Self-Assertion," also came under severe scrutiny, critique and challenge. Part of that critique runs thus:

> In the process [of producing a politically usable past], this analysis fell victim to the sins committed by colonial historiography—the sins of one-sidedness and idealization. The Africa that emerged out of this history was both ahistorical and asocial—ahistorical in the sense that it talked only of a glorious past uninterrupted by conflict and reversal and asocial in the sense that it failed

to deal with the social contradictions that drive all
social history.[5]

Whereas the European constructions of "Race" and the
"Civilizing Mission" had informed the former colonial historiography, the alleged "sins of one-sidedness and idealization"
in "The New Historiography" were informed by the values
of African Nationalism, Pan-Africanism, Negritude, Black
Consciousness, and the African Personality. These "sins of
one-sidedness and idealization," as E.J. Alagoa puts it, took
"the form of drum and trumpet glorification of ancient
African kingdoms and empires";[6] and, without a doubt, they
were also driven in part by a sense of race belonging and
Africa consciousness.

The latter exercise, like the one that preceded it, represented another example of the use and/or abuse of "evidence"
in the socio-cultural and political process of identity con-
struction- an inter-subjective activity in the scholastic business of knowledge production about Africa. By analyzing the
uses and/or abuses of evidence in the anti-black discourses
generated by the agents and philosophers of "race" and the
"civilizing mission" leading up to decolonization, including
the resistance narratives of the aforementioned anti-colonial
intellectuals of African descent, this essay intends to contribute substantially to the discourse on the politics of identity
construction as articulated by Kwame Anthony Appiah: "[I]
dentities are complex and multiple and grow out of a history
of changing responses to economic, political, and cultural
forces, almost always in opposition to other identities."[7] The
African self-image and identity, which the "Historiography of Self-Assertion" sought to create, for example, was in
ideological opposition to the one created and propagated by
the preceding colonial historiography; and it drew inspiration from the changing local and international forces that
challenged, undermined and eventually overthrew European
colonialism in Africa. Knowledge production about Africa

from the nineteenth century through to the attainment of independence from colonialism, as all of the foregoing introductory comments indicate, could not be disassociated from the global cultural and ideological politics of identity construction.

To methodologically present and analyze the aforementioned goals, the rest of the discussion will be given under these four related parts and/or headings. 1) Notions of Race and the Civilizing Mission. 2) Mapping Race and the Civilizing Mission as Outcomes of Global Historical Processes. 3) The Implications of Race and the Civilizing Mission for Framing Blackness and African Personhood following Colonization. 4) Concluding Comments: Combating European Constructions of Blackness and African Personhood—the Contributions of "The New African Historiography" or "The Historiography of Self-Assertion" after Independence. With these sub-themes, discussed separately and jointly, this essay will overall substantially reflect on the following forms of historical activity articulated by A.E. Afigbo: the discovery and critical analyzes of historical sources; the reconstruction and description of the subject being investigated on the basis of "evidence" or "facts" gleaned or quarried from the discovered sources; the construction, on the basis of these ascertained "facts" and/or "evidence," of some general theory that could give meaning and inner logic to the constructed narrative, as well as serving to educate society, or even helping to influence aspects of contemporary public policy or action; and, finally, reflecting on the trends and patterns of historical writing as they evolved over time on the subject being investigated.[8]

PART ONE
Notions of "Race" and the "Civilizing Mission"

I like to begin on the general note that "race," as a mythical concept and hegemonic narrative, has always been constructed or reconstructed, from time to time in modern history, for various self-serving ideological purposes by politically, militarily and economically powerful polities. Race narratives, as hegemonic constructs that change over time, are therefore designed to remold, redefine and nourish the sense of *self* (personhood), including the sense of group-identity and group-thinking prevailing among a people, with a view to, among other things, doing the following: denying equal social ranking, rights and privileges to all those creatures from less politically and economically powerful polities. Within modern democratic states, totalitarian kingdoms and empires, including non-centralized societies, the rule of "race" has always been used widely to enforce authority over slaves and subject peoples. For some four hundred years, for example, it was used on the American continent and its off-shore islands, including the Caribbean islands, to enforce the authority of those imputed white over those imputed black. Race, as an ideology of domination, exalted things European and demeaned things African; and, in order to differentiate whiteness from blackness, the peoples of African descent were methodically indoctrinated to despise their phenotype and African heritage under the rule of race in the Caribbean and the United States. The histories of slavery and the trans-atlantic slave trade in these slaveholding societies, where racial slavery was most rampant and practiced, profoundly influenced race thinking and also contributed immensely to the global ugly stigmatization of blackness and African personhood. Whiteness in these societies theoretically connoted freedom and riches, while blackness connoted servitude and shrill penury; and, as E.B. Rugemer puts it: black slavery was ideologically perceived as "a prop for white men's freedom" in these societies.[9] In the racialized mind of the slaveholders in the United States and the Caribbean, freedom was not a natural condition for Africans and their descendants; and, for this reason, it could therefore not be considered as their inalienable right. The opposition to the abolition of slavery, among other reasons, was based on the race-related thinking that emancipation could have far-reaching adverse implications for white-skin social and cultural privileges. Robert Monroe Harrison, the United States consul to Jamaica between 1831 and 1858, who was also an anti-abolitionist activist, bemoaned some of these adverse implications thus:

> Emancipation had instilled in the people a 'haughty behavior,' which resulted in various affronts. Jamaican blacks refused to 'pull their hats off when coming into a gentleman's house.' They always made 'a white man give way to them' when walking in the street and habitually insulted whites.[10]

While acknowledging and defining itself as a freedom-loving nation where "all men are created equal [and] endowed by their creator with certain inalienable rights," the slaveholding society of the United States of America denied African-Americans their full personhood. "America's founding elites," it is said, "had kept the Constitution free of the word slavery, but they had recognized the specific rights of slaveholders in manifold ways. As the years passed the basic obstacles to the opponents of slavery were racism and [capitalist] greed, which denied the full humanity of Africa's descendants...."[11] Legally defined as "property," and collectively perceived ideologically as "a prop for white men's freedom," African-Americans were not expected to partake in the Fourth of July Celebrations—white America's celebration of freedom from British colonialism. Hence non-conforming African-Americans, who had assembled in public spaces for this

Celebration, became the targets and victims of white-racist mob violence in the following cities: Philadelphia in 1805, New York in 1834, and Indianapolis in 1845.[12] Seen through the eyes of the slaveholders in these cities, the Fourth of July Celebrations and the values they represented were for only those imputed white. The emancipation of slaves, including the Thirteenth and Fourteenth Amendments to the American Constitution, brought very little cosmetic changes to the quality of existence that was centuries old and underwritten by the racist attitudes and practices of most whites. Through the Civil War to the mid-twentieth century, African-Americans were condemned under the rule of race in the North as well as in the South to a subordinate role within a preponderantly white culture.

Although the theoretical and empirical foundation of race discourse and thinking seemed dubious and weak from the outset, it was nevertheless generally accepted in Europe and in the United States, even by the critics of European empire building projects, as the basis for explaining differences between European and non-European populations in the world. With certain global socio-political developments before the end of the first half of the twentieth century, especially with the discovery of blood typing and the founding of genetics, "race" as an objective scientific concept or tool, came under serious scrutiny and relentless interrogation. It has since then been irreparably discredited and damaged by critics in the following disciplines, among others, in the last two decades of the previous century: biology, literary studies, history, social sciences, philosophy, and cultural studies. Race, many of these critics now contend, cannot explain observable human phenotypical, genotypical, and socio-cultural differences. It is, therefore, not a sound and logical basis for determining and constructing individual and group social identities, cultural affiliations, political movements, and public policies. Some of these critics have gone on to say that: "Racial identities and the forms of solidarity that they [allegedly] sustain are irrational, incoherent, rooted in illusions, or morally problematic."[13]

In nineteenth-century Western Europe and the United States, as hinted earlier, race narratives defined humanity in every sense and in every way conceivable because "race" was perceived and upheld as scientific, rational, and coherent. Race provided the set of self-serving ideological values that held together the various political, economic, religious, and socio-cultural networks constructed by the European imperialists in nineteenth-century Africa. European involvement in Africa during the second half of the nineteenth century, it has to be noted, has been generally described glowingly and approvingly as a "Civilizing Mission" by the apologists and protagonists of imperialism- for example, Joseph Chamberlain and Jules Ferry of Great Britain and France respectively. Since race defined humanity and influenced the formulation of domestic and foreign policies in nineteenth-century France and Victorian Britain, we may pause to ask these pertinent questions before proceeding. To what extent did it inform the construction of the "civilizing mission"? How does understanding "race" help us to better appreciate the ideological underpinnings of the "civilizing mission" it engendered and fostered? In raising and answering these questions, I intend to deal with the central aims of this paper initially declared; and to also interrogate, among other things, the notion that the "civilizing mission" was a calculated selfless, benign, and humanitarian desire to civilize, uplift, and economically develop non-European populations, including Africans.

Among European and African church historians, in particular those who have acknowledged that race and the civilizing mission had informed white/black relationships in the introduction, growth and development of the church and Christianity in Africa, the aforementioned questions are yet to be substantially and satisfactorily explored. Put differently the dialectic connections between race and the civilizing mission, including how these factors had influenced and shaped the evolving tumultuous white/black relationships within the various Christian missions in Africa, are sometimes misrepresented, downplayed, or even ignored, by some of these scholars. G.O.M. Tasie, for example, had criticized and sought to undermine or diminish the significance and emphasis E.A. Ayandele assigned to "race" as the most relevant and critical conceptual tool for framing, explaining, and comprehending the turbulent white-black relationship within the CMS Niger Mission in southern Nigeria during the last decade of the nineteenth century. According to Tasie: "[T]here were racial overtones" in the controversies that led to the formation and breaking away of the Niger Delta Pastorate Church in 1892 from the CMS Niger Mission, "but ... the race factor became so prominent because of the way the African agents [of the Niger Mission] overstated it."[14] In one of his essays on the civilizing mission- "The Cultural Factor in Victorian Imperialism: a case study of the British 'civilizing mission'"—D.M. Schreuder admittedly redressed some of the most glowing and praise-singing descriptions of the British "civilizing mission" from its secular and spiritual protagonists in the Cape Colony of South Africa; but he failed in his analysis to spotlight the critical and dialectic connections between those glowing descriptions and the prevailing notions of race and xenophobia in Victorian Britain during the nineteenth and early twentieth century.[15]

My central argument based on primary and published secondary data drawn from several works, including those of Phillip D. Curtin,[16] is that "race" engendered the "civilizing mission"; and, in unison, both forces worked together to construct and define "blackness" pejoratively in order to bolster and valorize the image of "whiteness" globally. How was that done? Here is one answer from Na'im Akbar, among many other answers to be discussed later.

> European-American people have done an admirable job of insuring that the content of their con-

sciousness was well informed about their greatness. The great stories of Louis XIV, Columbus,
Napoleon, Queen Victoria, Copernicus, Galileo,
the Greeks and the Romans are fundamental
elements of the information system that we are
given about European-American people. *This
barrage of information about European and American greatness is systematically given to themselves to
insure that they maintain their consciousness of who
they are.*[17] [My emphasis]

The making of a discourse of "race" in European and American societies, in a certain sense, revolved around one central
theme: identity construction. Conscious of themselves as the
makers of history, "race" and the "civilizing mission" persuaded
and emboldened Europeans to construct a lofty image and
identity for themselves while dehumanizing, vilifying, and
demonizing the "Others." Both forces, among other objectives, were aimed primarily at introducing and entrenching
white normativity globally: "[T]he centering of whiteness,"
to put it in the words of L.R. Gordon, "as the perspective on
and of reality."[18] Centering whiteness, simply put, involved
the restructuring of global reality around European experiences and expectations, accomplishments and values. The
nefarious transatlantic trade in enslaved Africans, including
the colonization of the continent that followed shortly after
the abolition of the slave trade, fashioned and facilitated the
tools, avenues and conditions for the restructuring of Africa's
image and identity by Europeans operating within and
outside of the continent.

As I have noted and discussed elsewhere,[19] it is theoretically and empirically difficult to discuss the civilizing mission
in isolation from race for these reasons. First, white supremacy from the outset of European involvement in Africa was
constitutive, not additive, to the makings of the civilizing
mission. Second, because the desire to enthrone whiteness

15

was constitutive to the makings of the civilizing mission from the outset, anti-black discourses in knowledge production were integral, not marginal, to the European colonial project in Africa. Third, as the next section will show, the very construction of "race" was a European creation rooted in attempts to rationalize the global social and psychological domination of non-European populations, particularly Africans, in the nineteenth and twentieth centuries.

The information that fed and nourished race thinking and the construction of the civilizing mission depended on a global system of data gathering and reporting about non-European cultures, and African cultures in particular, that began before the nineteenth century after the invention of printing. The first English newspapers, which appeared in the late 17th century, were official organs of the Crown. Before the end of the first half of the 18th century, however, a number of newspapers had appeared in metropolitan Britain, including the American colonies and the Caribbean. These pioneering newspapers, whose reporting reflected the "political geography" of the British Empire, laid the foundation for "the print culture of the Anglo-Atlantic world" that flourished in the 19th and 20th centuries.[20] That "print culture" vilified blackness in order to promote the civilizing mission.

Data gathering and reporting about non-European cultures largely depended on the activities and cultural networks engendered and sustained by European explorers, slave traders, missionaries, scientists, travelers, and adventurers. A mid-nineteenth century publication by Paul du Chaillu, *Explorations and Adventures in Equatorial Africa*, illustrates the point being made here. A review of that publication in a London newspaper, *The Times*, declared as follows:

> We must go back to the age of La Perouse and Captain Cook, and almost to the days of wonder, which followed the track of Columbus, for novelties of equal significance to the age of their discov-

ery. P. du Chaillu has struck into the torrid zone
from the western rivers, swamps and forests.[21]

That publication, we are told by the same source just cited, "sold ten thousand copies in two years at one guinea a copy" because it dealt with the curious subject of "a man-like ape that could walk on two legs," the gorilla. Africa, the continent of "novelties" and gorillas, provided fascinating data for "scientific racism" through the activities of explorers such as Chaillu, David Livingstone, Mungo Park, and Henry M. Stanley, just to mention a few. The explorations of Livingstone in Malawi, it has been noted, "led to Scottish missionaries settling there."[22] These agents of race and the civilizing mission generally reported, through print and museum exhibitions, what they perceived and construed as African "novelties" and "curiosities"—spectacular festivals, human sacrifices, judicial ordeals, and polygyny—that were culturally repugnant to their European populations while suppressing other more fundamental manifestations of a common humanity.

Through these agencies and the cultural and intellectual networks they generated and sustained, Europe began increasingly to engage race and the civilizing mission as the conceptual tools with which to frame, explain and comprehend its relationship with non-European peoples. These agents, and in particular the emergent colonial state after the Berlin Conference of 1884/5, became the propagators and torchbearers of whiteness in Africa. According to Charles Mills: "From about the beginning of the nineteenth century, or even earlier, race had become for Europeans the common conceptual denominator that gradually came to signify the respective global statuses of superiority."[23]

Race, in the words of Paul Gilroy, can be "constructively apprehended as a specific social product, the outcome of historical processes that can be mapped in detail."[24] The theoretical thinking underpinning this perception of race could be extended to include the civilizing mission; and I intend to argue that race and the civilizing mission are dialectically intertwining and interfacing social products, the outcomes of global historical processes that can be constructively apprehended and mapped in detail. Since race and the civilizing mission are dialectically related forms of consciousness in the overall development of Western European philosophical thought and civilization, mapping them together as outcomes of global historical processes could, arguably, also help us to illustrate an important philosophical proposition: "There is no consciousness without intentionality, where consciousness is consciousness *of* something, but 'something' cannot be apprehended without maintenance of it if but for a nanosecond."[25]

PART TWO

Mapping Race and the Civilizing Mission as Outcomes of Global Historical Processes

The makings of the contemporary ideas of "race" and "race" discourses are all historically traceable to the Enlightenment: "the harbinger of intellectual modernity" in Europe.[26] That "modernity," as it unfolded, also initiated, encouraged and fostered:

> a sustained inquiry on the European self, the con-
> sequence of which is, literally, *the European self.*
> Prior to such emergence, there was no self-identi-
> fied Europe. This process of forming the notion of
> a geopolitical self is, however, symbiotically linked
> to the negation of that self; that is to say that the
> process of determining "what" constitutes Europe
> and things European requires formulating what
> does *not* constitute such phenomena.[27]

In the process of determining "what" did not constitute the *European self* and "things European," Enlightenment philosophers divided humanity along racial lines.[28]

Also called the "Age of Reason," these philosophers— C. Montesquieu, F.M. Voltaire, J.J. Rousseau, C. Linnaeus, Comte de Buffon, D. Diderot, Immanuel Kant, and David Hume, among others—argued that only empirical studies based on reason and observation were critical to the understanding of the human social universe; and that all tangible, natural and social phenomena in the universe had been ordered according to discoverable, knowable, and testable general or covering laws. "The Enlightenment's declaration of itself," E.C. Eze has argued, as "'the Age of Reason' was predicated upon precisely the assumption that reason could historically only come to maturity in modern Europe, while the inhabitants of areas outside Europe, who were considered to be of non-European racial and cultural origins, were consistently described and theorized as rationally inferior and savage."[29]

Following the racial delineation of humanity there emerged the tendency, particularly during the Romantic Movement, to perceive social differences as natural and to rationalize and theorize them through the discourse of race. The Romantic Movement, it should be noted, even challenged some of the egalitarian and universalistic assumptions of the Enlightenment, while propagating the view that inequality was in the natural order of things. The works of Count Arthur Gobineau—*Essays on the Inequality of Races*— are classic illustrations of the concept of race informed by Romantic aristocratic reactions to Enlightenment values. For Gobineau, "all history was the history of racial struggle"; and "The basic organization and strength of all civilizations are equal to the traits and spirits of the dominant race."[30] It was Gobineau, benefiting in part from earlier works on the subject, who entrenched the notion of Aryan superiority: the blond, blue-eyed Nordic type as the natural aristocrat and the pinnacle of humanity. He went on to associate skin color with social rank, and presented dark-skinned people as servants of pale-skinned aristocrats. Both David Hume and Immanuel Kant, in discussing the differences between the developed European *self* and the undeveloped (not developing) African *selfhood*, also argued that: "they were substantial enough not to take seriously the status of blacks as human beings."[31] It was the collective writings of these men that engendered and also popularized the concept of "The Great Chain of Being"—a hierarchical social ordering or ranking of the various human races populating the planet.

There were those, it must be noted however briefly, who challenged the doubtful and spurious race data, including the empirical validity of the race theories, in the latter part of the nineteenth and early twentieth century—the heydays of "scientific racism." Franz Boas, for example, worked with others to show that variations in size, height, skin hues and eye colors, and even hair texture, existed within all human populations; and that these variations could also shift gradually from population group to population group, depending on the geographical locations and the climatic conditions.[32] They tried, but without success, to persuade Europe generally, and its political and race leaders in particular, to discard these race-oriented arguments as the most critical basis for constructing and organizing their relationships with non-European populations.

The European self-image, as portrayed in Africa during and after colonialism, could be traced back to the race thinking associated with, among others, Gobineau, Hume, and Kant. "Part of the self-image of the European in Africa," according to Terrence Ranger, "was his prescriptive right to have black servants."[33] European missionaries in the CMS Niger Mission in Southern Nigeria were provided with "very smart [black] boys, about ten to fourteen years of age, who do all the house work, at wages ranging from seven shillings six pence to ten shillings per month."[34] In addition, according to the same source just cited, whenever any European missionary needed to travel "any distance further than one can safely walk" he had "to use a hammock slung on a pole, and carried on the heads of four [black] men." Black servility, as we noted earlier in the slave holding societies of the United States, was also the "prop" for sustaining the ostentatious and opulent lifestyles Europeans generally enjoyed in colonial Africa. European missionaries, the denomination notwithstanding, undertook the cultural and social transformation of African societies on the race-oriented assumption that Africans were subpersons (It is very pertinent to keep this in mind as the essay unfolds). Owing to this perception, European missionaries constantly projected an aura of race preeminence, wittingly or unwittingly, in their dealings with Africans. In the church, as in the wider society, blackness generally meant servility.

"The Great Chain of Being," which hierarchically divided humanity on the basis of perceived and imagined racial differences in nineteenth-century European scientific and popular literature, had Europeans at the top and Africans at the bottom. All "light" peoples not originating from Europe—for example, the Chinese, Indians and Arabs, including the Berber populations of North Africa—were placed at the middle of this fictional and abominable hierarchical construction. These "light" Asiatic populations, the founders and propagators of Islam, Confucianism, and Buddhism, were recognized as possessing the attributes of civilization; as a result, they were not always overly described or perceived as very benighted and "primitive." Nevertheless, they were still considered as requiring Western tutelage for one principal reason: They "had been plunged for centuries in an obscurantism."[35] As a result of being plunged for centuries in this situation, according to James Norris Cheetham of the CMS Niger Mission, the Asiatic systems of philosophical thought and religions before and after Christianity can "only lift an ignorant people up to a certain distance, and then leave them in a kind of dream, in which they show

21

little of either the desire or the power to advance."[36] Donald Fraser of the United Free Church of Scotland also echoed the same sentiments when he argued that: "The Arab had no capacity for self-discipline and the idle luxury into which he sank when all labor was done for him by slaves, reduced his civilizing influence to the lowest degree."[37]

Fraser and Cheetham, who shared an identical race-oriented, Judeo-Christian worldview, had two things in common. First, they were expressing one of the most common and prevalent race-oriented assumptions that non-Western civilizations represented earlier stages of human progress that got frozen or fossilized at a point in time while the European world advanced.[38] Second, like James Stephen, the permanent under-secretary of the British Colonial Office from 1836 to 1847, they believed that "Christianity is the only religion ever known among men in strict alliance with philosophy, civilization and human advancement in all the arts and sciences."[39] James Cowles Pritchard, one of the writers on race in nineteenth-century Britain, also held one of the erroneously engrained common views about Islam that was very similar to those of Cheetham and Fraser earlier referred to. As he put it: Islam might awaken the faculties from the "brutal sloth of savage life," but at the same time render the morals "more depraved rather than improved."[40]

Because the civilizing influence of the Arabs and the Islamic religion they professed and propagated were considered to be of "the lowest degree," E.F. Gautier argued thus:

> North Africa experienced its most brilliant period of civilization in Roman and Christian antiquity, but it then became trapped in a historical oscillation between West and East and underwent a millennium of stagnation amid 'Islamic slumber,' and the European return in the form of colonization … made possible its regeneration.[41]

It is pertinent to mention that James Richardson, a British traveler in Africa who had witnessed and appreciated the Islamic civilizing influences in the Sahelian cities of Ghat and Ghadames, thought that the Arab world had contributed more to the civilization of Africa than Gautier would make us believe.[42] Richardson, including Boaz as noted earlier, represented an invisible and marginalized minority opinion that was undeserving of any serious political consideration and notice during this period—the period of global European triumphalism in science, technology, industry, and commerce.

During the course of the nineteenth and early twentieth century, in response to critics, those who advertised themselves as the disciples and followers of Locke and Montesquieu continued to make substantial contributions to the evolving self-serving discourse of "scientific racism" and the ideological values it promoted. Such contributions helped to strengthen and to sustain the growing conviction in Western minds of their race superiority generally, and the legitimacy of their nascent supremacist doctrines in particular. Ernest Renan argued, for example, that: "There is nothing shocking about the conquest of a country with an inferior race by a superior race that settles there to govern.... As much as conquest between races should be criticized, the regeneration of inferior or degenerate races by superior races is *the providential order of humanity*."[My emphasis][43] This became the moral and rational basis for the right of Europe to dominate the world; and, according to this rationality and providential philosophy, Europe possessed the right not only from God, but also from history and nature.

Ideologically motivated and empowered, European migrants felt at home everywhere in the world from the nineteenth century. The aim and purpose of European migrations into non-European territories, including Africa, went beyond the conquering, subjugating and civilizing of the so-called "degenerate and backward races." The exercise was also aimed at usurping and occupying territories that were perceived as empty and under-exploited for their natural resources. Since, according to Gobineau, "all history was the history of racial struggle," the resources of this world, and those of the conquered territories in particular, were there for the most resourceful, dynamic, enterprising and dominant race to exploit at the expense of the weaker races doomed inevitably for extinction. The nineteenth century, particularly the second half of that century, has been regarded as the age of European expansionism. This was, for example, amply illustrated by the scramble and partition of Africa between 1880 and 1900, including the earlier migrations of European populations into Australia, New Zealand, Canada, and North America.

Expansionism, and/or imperialism, was not simply an evocation of racial superiority; it was also expressed in terms of the civilizing mission. This was how Joseph Chamberlain, the Colonial Secretary of Great Britain, expressed it in 1897.

> You cannot have omelet without breaking eggs; you cannot destroy the practices of barbarism, of slavery, of superstition, which for centuries have desolated the interior of Africa, without use of force; but if you fairly contrast the gain to humanity with the price which we are bound to pay for it, I think you may well rejoice in the result.[44]

This notion of the "civilizing mission" [imperialism] as a moral crusade, or "the white man's burden," was firmly rooted in the notion of race and race narratives articulated and written by persons like Gobineau and Renan; and it was echoed throughout Europe, including North America. After the extermination of the Indians of North America, for example, Karl Pearson noted that: "although the Europeans had certainly had to wipe out whole tribes the final outcome 'has given us a good far outbalancing its immediate evil.'"[45] G.W.F. Hegel, a nineteenth-century historian and philosopher, race activist and thinker, also had this to say about European emigration to America.

*Since the original American nation has vanished—or as good as vanished—*the effective population comes for the most part from Europe, and everything that happens in America has its origin there. The surplus population of Europe has emigrated to America, by a process not unlike that which occurred in former times in the imperial German cities.

> America has also become a place of refuge for the dregs of European society. Indeed, emigration to America offers many advantages, for the emigrants have cast off much that might restrict them at home, and they bring with them the benefits of European self-reliance and European culture without the accompanying disadvantages; and to those who are willing to work hard and who have not found an opportunity to do so in Europe, America certainly offers ample scope.[46][My emphasis]

The members of the "original American nation" referred to, it should be recalled and reemphasized, were systematically destroyed and eliminated through the predatory activities of the incoming Europeans.

In July 1885 (after the Berlin West African Conference and long after the French *Declaration of the Rights of Man and the Citizen*) Jules Ferry of France, like Joseph Chamberlain of Great Britain, argued thus: "There is a law for the superior races because there is a duty for them. They have the duty of civilizing the inferior races."[47] That "law for the superior races," it may be noted, had guaranteed the right to liberty, religious freedom and thought, equal treatment before the law, promoted the rights of ordinary people and also brought attention to the demands of the poor, among many other democratic values. These were some of the democratic reforms and benefits of the French Revolution; and they soon became a model and inspiration for change among "the superior races" inhabiting Europe and North America.

By some twisted extension of the prevailing race thinking informing that "law for the superior races," however, imperial France found the moral and legal conscience, including the anthropological arguments, to deny all of the aforementioned freedoms to the "inferior races" of Africa during its civilizing mission to the continent. Clearly the French *Declaration of the Rights of Man and the Citizen*, like the "Fourth of July Celebrations" in the United States earlier referred to in Part One of this essay, were never meant for the "inferior races." Grounding the legitimacy of its imperial project on the intertwined ideas of racial superiority and the civilizing mission, France proceeded to urge its population to occupy its North African conquered territories at the expense of the indigenous Arabo-Berber populations.

> Tunisia [in North Africa] offers a vast field for the activity of our fellow-countrymen. A farmer now vegetating on a little property without any hope of expanding it ... will find across the Mediterranean the means of giving his life a broader horizon. A large property-owner will find in colonization the means of lessening the impact of inheritance legislation, for he will be able to keep his whole estate in the hands of one of his children if, during his lifetime, he makes the moderate sacrifice of giving the others the means later to become landowners in Tunisia. It is impossible ... to list all the advantageous combinations that ... a colony whose good repute becomes daily apparent can offer to well-advised individuals.[48]

All of the aforementioned excerpts taken from Chamberlain, Hegel, and Ferry, make it succinctly and abundantly clear that the civilizing mission was an integral part of the evolving "racial contract" between Europeans and non-European populations whose general purpose, as articulated by Charles Mills, was to legitimate "the differential privileging of the Europeans as a group, with respect to the [non-European populations] as a group, the exploitation of their [souls through the missionaries], bodies, land, and resources, and the denial of equal socioeconomic opportunities to them."[49]

Through the evolving discourse of race and the civilizing mission, Europe was proclaimed and exalted as the secular and spiritual arm of "progress"; and most Europeans were encouraged to perceive their own way of life (whiteness) as representing values worthy of universal application. The nineteenth-century European philosophers, who articulated the idea of "progress," also attempted to persuade the rest of humanity to accept its inevitability as defined and prescribed by them. It should be noted that the inevitability of change and progress, which they articulated, was based on a teleological interpretation of human development that was unidirectionally moving towards the triumph of civilization. That civilization was, for the uncritical and ardent apostles and philosophers of race and the civilizing mission, the nineteenth century contemporary European society founded on Judeo-Christian values and the values of capitalism.

Free trade, the hallmark of capitalism, was perceived during the colonial era as a way of showing benighted Africans the economic benefits of advanced European technologies and the social relations of production they have engendered through an efficient international division of labor. These comments associated with Thomas Carlyle, a proslavery activist in Britain during the mid-nineteenth century, represented one of the commonplace derogatory views about the attitude of Africans to work:

> "[B]lacks would not work unless forced to do so;
> it is congenital. Britain's experiment with freedom
> in the West Indies had shattered abolitionist the-

> ories by demonstrating *that blacks did not respond to free labour incentives.* Their physical needs were pumpkin and rum, and once those were obtained, *they preferred idleness.* Blacks had only one right, 'the indisputable and perpetual right to be compelled' to labour. [My emphasis][50]

It was felt that for Africa to fulfill its envisaged historic role, as the supplier of raw materials in the evolving global production relations driven by capitalism and the "racial contract," it has to embrace the European work philosophy; and there has to be a massive socio-cultural transformation of its indigenous workforce through Christianity and Western education.

Work, in the context of the European civilizing mission during the colonial era, was presented as a moral and ideological force capable of "ennobling a man's character." In 1878 Anthony Trollope, while discussing the "famed Kimberley diamond diggings" of South Africa, had also taken time to comment on the prevailing Victorian notion that "work is the great civiliser of the world."

> Who can doubt that work is the great civiliser of the world? If there be one who does, he should come to see how those dusky troops of labourers, who until ten years ago were living in the wildest state of unalloyed savagery, whose only occupation was the slaughter of each other in tribal wars, each of whom was slave to his chief, who were subject to the dominion of the most brutalizing and cruel superstitions, have already put themselves on the path towards civilization....[51]

All the colonial powers, based on this race-related reasoning, had rationalized their unbridled and selfish exploitation of African labour as an attempt to purge the "idleness [that] keeps [the African] in a state of absolute economic inferiority."[52] In this respect, legitimate commerce and the unequal capitalist terms of exchange it fostered, the exploitative business of engaging forced and/or underpaid African wage labour on European owned plantations and mining companies, including Christianity and Western education that devalued things African, were all perceived and upheld ideologically as the avenues for promoting European values in the continent. Hence the ultimate aim of race and the civilizing mission, however they may be discredited, construed and perceived by their critics and the critics of empire, was to spread Western values in order to produce a benign convergence of societies across the planet. The civilizing mission, arguably, was a force for globalization in the nineteenth century; and its agents, in pursuit of the three Cs—Christianity, Legitimate Commerce and Civilization—in Africa, could also be construed as the forerunners of present-day globalization in the continent.

Aside from the colonial state, the Christian missions, and the chartered trading and mining companies, those who undertook to globalize Western values also included those Europeans who had individually migrated from Europe for various reasons during the nineteenth and twentieth centuries.

> From 1830 to 1920 more than 35 million Europeans set sail for the United States, including 4.5 million British, 4.6 million Irish, 2.5 million Scandinavians, 6.5 million Germans, nearly 1 million Poles, some 4 million subjects of the Russian Empire, and 5 million Italians.
>
> As to the other major destinations of the exodus, 8 million people arrived in Canada in the course of the nineteenth century, and between 1820 and 1940 a little over 2 million Europeans chose to settle in Australia, while some 12 million Italians, Spanish, Portuguese and Germans set off for South America and hundreds of thousands for the African colonies. Altogether more than

60 million Europeans left their native continent
in a little more than a century—the equivalent of
14 per cent of the population of Europe in 1914.[53]

Because these migrating populations believed that they had
"the duty of civilizing the inferior and degenerate races" on
"The Great Chain of Being," including the related supremacist belief that there could be "nothing shocking about the
conquest of a country with an inferior race by a superior
race that settles to govern," the civil and human rights of
the indigenous populations were generally greeted and
treated with great ignominy and were also given very scant
regard. Their physical survival as a social and cultural group,
for the same reasons, was very easily and readily subsumed
to the self-centered socioeconomic goals of the migrants
from Europe. The architectural settlement patterns and
arrangements of the migrating populations from Europe
also brutally interfered with the settlement patterns of the
indigenous populations. John T. Thomson, New Zealand's
first surveyor-general, for example, "believed that the extinction of the indigenous population was a precondition for the
modernization of [that country]."[54]

Given this obnoxious supremacist worldview of the
settlers, the cultural politics of color bar and racial exclusion became a way of life in South Africa, New Zealand,
Canada, North America, and Australia. "The 1890s and the
first decade of the twentieth century," according to K. Malik,
"were the age of immigration control in these territories."[55]
In 1896, for example, with a view to creating a "white Australia," several states in Australia passed the "Colored Races
Restriction and Regulation Acts" to alienate and marginal-
ize the native inhabitants of Asia, Africa, and the Pacific
islands. Canada, in order to create "white Canada," enacted
the Immigration Act of 1910 to prohibit, as they put it, the
entry "of immigrants belonging to any race deemed unsuit-
able to the climate or requirements of Canada." Finally, the

attempt to create "white South Africa" attracted the following approving comments from the *London Times* in September 1910: "[T]he brown, black and yellow races of the world"
have to realize that "inequality is inevitable ... not due to
inferior status but to the facts of race."[56]

The policy of territorial and residential segregation of
people in South Africa was based on the race reasoning
that black and white communities have different wants and
requirements socio-economically, culturally, and politically.
In the eyes of the apartheid state of South Africa, therefore:
"The mixing up of two such alien elements as white and
black leads to unhappy social results—racial miscegenation,
moral deterioration of both, racial antipathy and clashes, and
to many other forms of social evil."[57] This essentialist view of
race, as the basis for community organization and the determination of status and identity, including the construction
of socio-cultural affiliation and belonging, was also very pervasive in the Southern States of America between 1880 and
the first half of the twentieth century- the era of the "Civil
Rights Movement." According to Alan Conway:

> By 1910 it was estimated that in the majority
> of Southern States the Negro vote had virtually
> been eliminated. State racists capped the process
> by enacting the harsh segregation 'Jim Crow' laws
> throughout the South which gave quasi-legality
> to the doctrines of white supremacy and Negro
> inferiority. When even the Supreme Court in the
> landmark case of *Plessy versus Ferguson* in 1896
> gave its constitutional blessing to the 'separate but
> equal' doctrine and upheld segregation in trans-
> portation and education, the opening was pro-
> vided for individual states to extend segregation
> by discrimination into every aspect of Southern
> life. This final capitulation to racism made any
> white man superior to any Negro. The coloured
> man thus found himself in constant jeopardy and

lynchings increased apace—with over 3,000 cases being recorded between 1880 and 1900.[58]

Enoch Powell, a rightwing politician, represented those who endorsed the essentialist notion of race in Great Britain. In 1968, for example, he had argued that: "A West Indian or an Asian does not by being born in England become an Englishman. In law he becomes a United Kingdom citizen by birth; in fact he is a West Indian or an Asian still."[59] Britishness or Englishness, according to this essentialist view, is genetic; and it cannot, therefore, be acquired culturally or politically. Here is a first-hand experiential account of a West Indian in mid-twentieth century London, Geoff Henry Palmer, about the efforts of Powell and his ideological allies to "Keep Britain White."

> [W]e arrived in London where the 'Keep Britain White' graffiti confirmed general antipathy to our colour and as some newspapers fanned the flames of prejudice, the 'Black Shirts' and others attacked us. Two politicians were particularly unpleasant. Powell despised us because we, a tiny powerless minority, would somehow cause 'rivers of blood.' Nabarro, a comparatively recent Citizen of the Empire, cynically resurrected the slave-derived propaganda of 'the dangers of black sexuality.' With unbridled hate he stated that white girls would destroy their families' well- being by taking home big black men to tea.[60]

Palmer, who later became a professor of Grain Science "at a University near Edinburgh," argued that: "The original concept of Britishness was not about skin colour, it was [rather] about a family of different people who shared a political history that emanated from Britain."[61] "The original concept of Britishness," as articulated by Professor Palmer, reinforces the view that "race" is an ideological construction to rationalize the social and psychological domination of non-European populations; and the civilizing mission was a culturally crafted instrument for achieving and advancing the objectives of race during the phase of European expansion into non-European societies. Put simply, the notion of Britishness, like other forms of identities such as Frenchness and Americaness, was deliberately reconstructed over time to exclude certain human population groups for socioeconomic and political reasons, among others.

Race and the civilizing mission, as Europeans expanded their horizon beyond the geographical boundaries of the European continent and confronted an amazing and complex diversity of human populations and cultures, became the veritable ideological tools for remolding their own personhood and identity at the expense of the "other" races populating the world. In constructing the new European *self*, all "other" races on "The Great Chain of Being" were, in varying degrees, perceived and described as subhuman or not fully human. "Subpersons," in the words of C.W. Mills, "are humanoid entities who, because of racial phenotype/genealogy/culture, are not fully human and therefore have a different and inferior schedule of rights and liberties applying to them."[62] In the "Geographical Basis of World History," Hegel had argued for "a different and inferior schedule of rights and liberties" for Africans because, among other reasons: [The African] knows nothing of an absolute being [the Judeo-Christian God] which is other and higher than his own self." "The Negro," as a result of this ignorance, "is an example of *animal man* in all his savagery and lawlessness, and if we wish to understand him at all, we must put aside all our European attitudes."[63] [My emphasis] These "European attitudes," secular and spiritual, constituted the hallmarks of civilization for Hegel. For Hegel and other race thinkers of the late nineteenth and early twentieth century, there was an immense cultural and psychological gulf that separated the European from the superstition-ridden African, with his almost total ignorance of the connection between cause and effect.

The pervasive race thinking that the Negro "is an example of animal man," who is yet to become fully human because of his total ignorance of the connection between cause and effect, might have encouraged the formulation of the infamous "System of Negro Jurisprudence." "The leading idea in the Negro System of Jurisprudence," according to the document summary given in 1789 by the Clerk of the British Committee on the Slave Trade, "is that ... Negroes were property, and a species of property that needed a rigorous and vigilant regulation."[64] My point is that the banal commodification of enslaved Africans, including the imposition of the civilizing mission on the continent after the era of legal enslavement, cannot be disassociated from the subpersonhood status generally assigned to Africans by European race thinkers.

European expansion in the nineteenth and twentieth centuries, inspired and underpinned by the interlocking concepts under discussion, glorified and globalized those "attitudes" that constituted "whiteness." Jules Ferry, for instance, had urged France in the last quarter of the nineteenth century to export "wherever it could, its language, its customs, its flag, its arms and its genius"[65] in order to promote and universalize its self-image. The French colonial administrative policy of *Assimilation* in West Africa between 1891 and 1960, it may be recalled, was ideologically driven by the desire to promote Frenchness based on the ideas of imperialists like Ferry. On the basis of the foregoing empirical data drawn across the globe, the following related points could be made safely about race and the civilizing mission: first, they can be apprehended and mapped as intertwining and interfacing social products; second, they are the outcomes of historical processes; and, third, they were designed and intended to legitimize European world domination. Both concepts attempted to justify Western Europe's misuse of "evidence" and the principle of "might is right" in its relationship with militarily weaker non-European peoples; this is because, as

S. Bessis puts it: "The West seems to have too lofty an idea of itself to make brute force and [economic] self-interest the only reasons for its endeavors."[66]

These interlocking concepts, as the next part will show more fully, constituted the means of political and social control in colonial Africa after the Berlin West African Conference of 1884/5. They constituted the standard means by which authority was exercised in every European colony—settler or non-settler—in the continent. The rule of race and the civilizing mission, at the expense of sounding monotonous, was aimed at accomplishing one thing ideologically: the underdevelopment of blackness. Africans as subpersons, in the process of expanding whiteness, were expected to keep silence, listen to their European overlords, copy their examples, and give up on their benighted indigenous socio-cultural values and religions. Brainwashed Africans and overzealous new converts to Christianity in English-speaking territories, and in particular those being prepared for *assimilation* in the French-speaking territories, were expected with docility and gratitude to become perfect or near perfect "photographic negatives of the colonizers." That expectation, for some European critics of the civilizing mission, was however considered unattainable for one principal reason: no amount of training could make the African a European; and, on the other hand, no amount of deficiency of culture could make the European an African. This kind of race thinking echoes "the woad policy" that was adopted by the British Colonial Office during the interwar period: the African, according to that "policy," was *essentially* a different type of human being from the European; and, therefore, should be left to develop his own type of institutions in his own way. The British colonial policy of Indirect Rule in Africa was in part informed by this essentialist notion of race.

PART THREE

The Implications of Race and the Civilizing Mission for Framing Blackness and African Personhood following Colonization

Before the second half of the nineteenth century Europe's attempts at dominating the world had produced a knowledge system that theoretically legitimized the colonial adventures and economic exploits of Europeans in Africa. That system engendered and fostered a certain consciousness among all Europeans in Africa, including African missionaries such as Bishop S.A. Crowther of the CMS Niger Mission in southern Nigeria, to pursue the following agenda methodically: the elevation of whiteness over blackness, the devaluation of black and/or African personhood, and the simultaneous promotion of the attributes of European selfhood.

Race, in colonial Africa, constituted a group identity that sought to confer   predetermined socioeconomic, political and cultural advantages and privileges on Europeans. This was demonstrated in the entire continent, particularly in the settler colonies of South Africa, Algeria, Kenya, and Zimbabwe. In these settler colonies, wages, residential locations, and settlement patterns, including access to education, healthcare, and recreation, were predetermined by race and the requirements of the civilizing mission. Colonialism, founded on race assumptions, persuaded all Europeans to maintain an aura of race preeminence and class snobbery so as not to lose face or prestige in front of their benighted African subjects. In 1917, for example, while responding to a petition from black West Indian missionaries against the differential privileging of Europeans as a group within the CMS Niger Mission in southern Nigeria, Sidney Smith (the Mission's European secretary) said:

> I feel strongly that while I value the West Indians and appreciate their work as much if not more than anyone. I would not be prepared to make any radical changes [to the conditions of their contract with the Niger Mission] in order to keep them in our service if by so doing the status of these men [and women] becomes for all practical purposes that of European missionaries.[67]

In a separate report from Smith written and designed to defend and protect "white-skin privileges," as Appiah[68] calls them, he had declared that: "West Indians however good they may be can never take the place of Europeans."[69] Under the terms of the "racial contract" with non-European populations, Smith appears to have taken his white personhood for granted; and, operating from that ideological vantage point, he had perceived black West Indians as subpersons entitled only to subordinate positions—drawers of water and hewers of wood. To put the matter more squarely in the words of Charles W. Mills, "race" was being used by the management of the CMS Niger Mission as "the marker of entitlement or dispossession ... normative inclusion or ... exclusion, full or diminished personhood."[70] Smith's comments, seen at another related level of thought analysis articulated by P. Gilroy, meant that: "Racially differentiated [black populations] no longer shared the same present [with the dominant European group]. [The latter could, therefore,] enlist the irresistible momentum of history on their side and treat their apparently anachronistic subordinates as if they belong to the past and had no future."[71]

Before the Second World War, all of the colonial powers believed that European rule in Africa would last forever because they had perceived and treated the subjugated Africans as anachronistic subordinates who belonged to the past and had no future. Such attitudes arose naturally from the thinking that it would take the African a very long time, if indeed it were within his capacity given his perceived backwardness, to travel the entire distance from the Stone Age to twentieth-century civilization. These were some of the damning exposures of European attitudes of superiority, race snobbery and imperial arrogance toward their African colonies. "Enlisting," to once more use the words of Gilroy, "the irresistible momentum of history on their side" France under De Gaulle punished Guinea-Conakry in 1958 for severing links with its colonial master: between 1958 and 1960, France excluded Guinea-Conakry from the franc zone after withdrawing all French civil servants within two months of Guinea-Conakry becoming independent. White Rhodesians (Zimbabwe), similarly refusing to acknowledge the inevitability of black rule and the prospects of subordinating Europeans to a government led by blacks, unilaterally declared that country's independence in 1965 under Ian Smith. Both Smith and De Gaulle were saying the same thing philosophically: in the context of race rule in Africa, racially differentiated black populations could "no longer share the same present" with the dominant European groups.

The aforementioned plight of the black West Indians in the Niger Mission was not without precedent in the unfolding racialized relationship between the CMS and its African adherents in southern Nigeria. In 1844 Henry Venn, the secretary of the CMS establishment at Salisbury Square in London, had justified the wage gap between the racially differentiated employees of the Yoruba Mission workforce— Europeans and Africans- on the following considerations. First, the African employees, their qualifications and work experiences notwithstanding, needed to remain "near the material level of their fellow countrymen." Second, the CMS also needed to avoid "promoting self-indulgence" among its African employees.[72] These comments demonstrate very clearly that, even in the religious department of the civilizing mission, exploitation was rife and there was no racial equality. European missionaries always sought to maintain an aura of race preeminence in their relationship with Africans within and outside of the Christian faith community.

The "white man's burden" or the civilizing mission in Africa was succinctly expressed in Article Six of the *General Act* of the Berlin Conference of 1885, which delineated the continent among these nineteenth century European imperial overlords: Britain, France, Germany, Portugal, Belgium, Italy, and Spain.

> All powers exercising sovereign rights or influence in the said territories undertake to preserve the native peoples and to improve their moral and material conditions of existence.... They shall protect and promote all institutions and enterprises ... *tending to educate the natives and to make them understand and appreciate the advantages of civilization.*[73][My emphasis]

Through the colonial self-sacrifice of Europeans, as the above excerpt suggests, it was believed that inferior and primitive races in Africa south of the Sahara, including those possessing some (but not all) of the attributes of civilization, such as the Islamized Berbers of North Africa, could become part of a civilized humanity under Western tutelage.

For some reasons not worth detailing and discussing here, there were a few dissenting European voices within and outside of Europe against the civilizing mission. Sir William Lawrence, the author of *Lectures on Physiology, Zoology, and the Natural History of Man*, argued thus:

> Rather let them remain forever in a state of contented barbarism, than by civilizing their minds, only awaken them to a bitter consciousness of their fate; or by polishing their manners render them susceptible of desires, which you never mean to gratify.[74]

E.D. Morel, according to J.N. Cheetham, had argued slightly differently from Lawrence's perspective and position thus: "Native life is interfered with by the missionary propaganda; that its unity is destroyed; and that the result of our work is to 'Europeanize' the people and make them to be out of touch with their fellows and disloyal to their chiefs."[75] Morel, it should be recalled, was a trader in West Africa and a social commentator during the second half of the nineteenth century. One thing, however, readily reconciled the antagonists and protagonists of the civilizing mission throughout the nineteenth and early twentieth century: overwhelming faith in the intertwined elements of race and imperial pride.

In an apparent celebration of race success mingled with imperial pride in the last decade of the nineteenth century, Joseph Chamberlain, Britain's Colonial Secretary, had summarized the accomplishments of the civilizing mission to Africa in this way.

> Our rule does, and has, brought security and peace and comparative prosperity to countries that never knew these blessings. In carrying out this work of civilization we are fulfilling what I belief to be our national mission, and we are finding scope for the exercise of those faculties and qualities, which have made us a great governing race. [Indeed], the British race is the greatest race that the world has ever seen.[76]

The missionaries of the CMS Niger Mission in southern Nigeria fully endorsed this evaluation of the civilizing mission and the expressions of jingoism by Chamberlain. Africans, in the race thinking of both Chamberlain and these CMS missionaries, were only potential *persons* because they were deemed benighted and morally depraved. However (and this was part of the race thinking that ideologically united Chamberlain and the CMS missionaries), these potential

persons (the benighted and morally depraved Africans) could ultimately achieve the status of personhood if they were sufficiently transformed to exercise their moral capacities according to the doctrines and teachings of Christianity under the aegis of British colonial rule. Like Chamberlain, J.N. Cheetham (the Mission's chief accounting officer), had also argued thus: "[N]o other body of men on the face of the earth could provide a better administrative force for Nigeria than the British Government."[77] Given this common sense of race pride mingled with jingoism, it was not surprising that the CMS missionaries generally recommended obedience to colonial regulations while proselytizing in southern Nigeria. In fact, in addition to their missionary work, some of them deemed as "experts" on African affairs– for example, Cheetham and G.T. Basden—were invited to serve in the colonial administration.

Promoting the tripartite forces of race, imperial pride, and the civilizing mission, to use the words of T. Ballantyne, depended on "an imperial knowledge system."[78] To some degree, that "imperial knowledge system" had encouraged the verbal ideological manipulation, representation (or misrepresentation) of "facts," the museum ordering (or reordering) of historical, anthropological and ethnographic "evidence," including a sustained and relentless print attack at African personhood and blackness, during the period under review. With the advantages of printing technology available to Europeans, coupled with the global economic prosperity before the two decades (1861-1891) of recession in the second half of the nineteenth century, agents of race and the civilizing mission—missionaries, consular officials of the Crown, explorers, adventurers, scientists, and traders—were able to create and foster the requisite social and intellectual networks that enhanced the mass production, exchange and consumption of ethnographic and anthropological materials about the continent of Africa, its peoples, and cultures.

Print generally fostered and nourished a growing metropolitan interest in the activities of European empires overseas—for example, those of France and Britain in Africa. Among the economically buoyant metropolitan middle and upper classes in Britain, as I noted earlier in "Part One," there began a strong and avid demand for travel writings, narratives of exploration and imperial adventures, highlighting "native customs" in the nineteenth century. "These popular travel writings," it has been observed, also "contributed significantly to the perception of Europe as familiar and 'civilized,' living in the Age of Light, while the peoples of other lands (Asia, Africa, and America) were of 'strange' habits and mores. Savagery could then be physically located outside of Europe, outside of light, so that Africa, for example, was considered the Dark Continent, and the *terra nulla*."[79]

In addition to these travel writings, evangelical magazines also contributed to the image of Europeans as those "living in the Age of Light." Racialized accounts of the trials of missionaries in the remote mission fields scattered across Africa, in particular stories about the "strange habits and mores" of the benighted indigenous populations in the continent, were circulated within the British Empire to reinforce and underscore the differences between the European *self* and the subpersonhood ascribed to Africans. Here is one horrifying example published in 1932 by the *Jamaica Diocesan Magazine*—an official magazine of the Church of England in Jamaica.

> A plaintive wail, and lo! Another little life has been launched into this world. But alas! What is this? No smuggling of the little child into nice warm clothing, but instead something stands ready with a sharp razor!
>
> Not indeed to end the infant's life by violence but to do something, which often results in death all the same. For the tender little body just born is

> shaved all over and then the little one is placed for
> hours in cold water to shiver and to wail! Some-
> times pneumonia follows this terrible exposure
> and the frail little life is ended almost as soon as
> it has begun. Where is it that such a barbarous
> thing can be, you ask? It is happening today in
> West Africa. *Remember every penny you collect ...*
> *will ensure some precious babe a better chance to live,*
> *a better opportunity to learn of God, and best of all*
> *to know the love of the Lord Jesus for every little*
> *child.*[80][My emphasis]

Most missionary organizations failed to discourage this
kind of horrifying and sensational reporting in order to raise
funds for their civilizing projects in non-European societies,
including Africa. Missionaries were in fact, as Article VIII
of the Wesleyan Methodist "Instructions to Missionaries"
indicates, advised or encouraged to produce "interesting"
(sensational) reports for the delightful consumption of "the
friends of the Missions at home."

> It is peremptorily required of every missionary in
> our connexion to keep a journal, and to send home
> frequently such copious extracts of it as may give
> full and particular account of his labours, success,
> and prospects. He is required to give such details
> of a religious kind, as may be generally interesting
> to the friends of the Missions at home; particu-
> larly accounts of conversion.[81]

The Church Missionary Society also had a similar require-
ment for their missionaries; and the organization also published a range of printed materials designed to inform [or
misinform] and educate [or mis-educate] its supporters in
the United Kingdom: *The Church Missionary Record, The*
Church Missionary Intelligencer, The Juvenile Instructor, and
the *CMS Quarterly Paper.*

Propagandistic stories, such as the piece rendered in the *Jamaican Diocesan Magazine*, are therefore copious and replete in both colonial and missionary archives; and they were intended to present carefully constructed images of the Empire's indigenous savage populations in order, among other things, to impress upon the British people the race preeminence of their global Empire and the humanitarian and selfless values underpinning its civilizing mission. Above everything else, these accounts were also aimed at emphasizing the global views of difference, and they constituted the sources of information for all those engaged in the making of the evolving discourse of race and the civilizing mission in the nineteenth and twentieth centuries. Hegel, for example, "had available to him a far greater amount of anthropological reports from missionaries and explorers than any of his predecessors."[82]

The critical role of print—secular and evangelical—in the dissemination of whiteness has been illustrated above from two related perspectives: as an instrument within the "ritual" of communication through which an entire community could become ideologically connected and defined; and as a "transmitter" that carries news or ideas from one place to another for the consumption of any interested persons. Missionary organizations, including imperial government agencies within and outside of Europe, through museum ethnographic displays of handicrafts collected from different parts of world, also portrayed the global views of difference during the nineteenth and early twentieth centuries to both their loyal and doubting audiences. The latter included the critics of empire, race, and the civilizing mission. Here, for example, is an instructive and revealing report published in the *Jamaica Times* on "The Missionary Exhibition" held under the auspices of the Church of England in Jamaica in May 1910. It was definitely calculated to illustrate cultural differences between Asia and Africa, with a view to justifying the civilizing mission to the latter continent under the aegis of the Church of England in Jamaica. But it could also, wittingly or unwittingly, further legitimize and reinforce Asia's race-oriented ranking ahead of Africa on the "The Great Chain of Being."

> In the Chinese, Japanese and East Indian sections [of "The Missionary Exhibition"], visitors had an opportunity of seeing something of these older forms of civilization to which the Christian Missionary bears the Gospel Message. This is very different to that of West Africa or East Africa. To many of those who attended the exhibition the fine handicraft of the Japanese, the Hindu and Chinese, in all sorts of metal work and woodcarving, must have come as a revelation. *The ruder work of West Africa has a special interest in view of the intimate relation between that part of Africa and the West Indies.*[83] [My emphasis]

Such displays provided exceedingly appropriate contexts for exploring the "poetics of exhibition": that is, the practice of creating meaning through the juxtaposing of separate but related exhibition items. This practice, Ballantyne has noted, had the immediate effect of making "ethnographic knowledge accessible"; and the huge audiences they attracted in the United Kingdom and Jamaica also reflected "the growing popularity of empire as a theme of entertainment." Finally, because these exhibitions made the world "smaller," "accessible" and "digestible," they enabled European metropolitan audiences, including those audiences in the colonial peripheries such as Jamaica, "'to take an excursion around the world.'"[84] These "excursions" strengthened the political and moral support for the "civilizing mission" and the British Empire at large.

Secular sociopolitical organizations, which were interested in the empire-building project that was based on propagating and exalting whiteness at the expense of blackness, also tried to maximize the advantages of print. This may be illustrated by the amount of publications—ranging from fiction to scientific and academic literature—on Africa, and on the related sub-theme of African subpersonhood, produced during the first half of the nineteenth century.

> Over four hundred books and articles were published in the West by 1800 and another three hundred by 1865 on West and West Central Africa. The figures for Southern Africa were about the same up to 1865, but higher for the rest of the nineteenth century. Lower numbers of publications were made for Central Africa before 1800. The quantity of published materials for East Africa was lower than for West Africa before 1865, but leveled up from about that date.[85]

These ethnographic and anthropological monographs, according to E.J. Alagoa, did not [and were not intended to] enhance the understanding of African history because "the [race-oriented] paradigm of social Darwinism [had] provided the framework for most of these writings."[86] In fact, the historiography that emanated from the West, in the period immediately preceding the abolition of the transatlantic trade in enslaved Africans and the European colonization of the continent, attempted to articulate two related themes in the cultural framing of African personhood and blackness: the theories of primitive and savage peoples without history—as exemplified by the writings of G.W.F Hegel, A.P. Newton, and H. Trevor Roper—and the theories of Hamitic motivation—as exemplified by the separate writings of G.T. Basden, C.G. Seligman, H.H. Simpson, and Joseph. J. Williams.

Linguistics, anthropology, sociology, philosophy, surveying, cartography, and biology, among other disciplines, facilitated the ideological project of European empire building in nineteenth and early twentieth century Africa and also devalued blackness and African personhood. All of these disciplines, especially history as defined by Euro-centric scholars, endorsed the view that "progress" and "reason" were the prerogatives of the Aryan master race at the top of "The Great Chain of Being." At the intellectual level these disciplines could be regarded as the "tools for empire building" and the "instruments for sustaining imperialism" thereafter. For example, regional, divisional, and district geographical boundaries within the nascent colonies of the empire, including primary producing communities of strategic mineral resources and agricultural commodities, were identified and mapped through surveying and ethnographic investigations. Among other uses, data from these investigations also facilitated the effective engagement of colonial military forces against African resistance movements during the early twentieth century.

Philosophy and history in particular, like missionary Christianity, attempted to justify the conquest of Africa and the imposition of the civilizing mission on its populations. Like Christianity, these disciplines, separately and jointly, made their contributions to the glamorization of whiteness and the vilification of blackness. In *The Philosophy of History* G.W.F. Hegel stated, for example, that: "Africa is no historical part of the world" because "it has no movement or development to exhibit. Historical movements in it—that is, in its northern part—belong to the Asiatic and European world.... What we properly understand by Africa is the unhistorical, undeveloped spirit, still involved in the conditions of mere nature, and which had to be presented here only as on the threshold of the world's history."[87] A.P. Newton and Hugh Trevor-Roper represented twentieth-century readings on the above perception of Africa and its peoples south of the Sahara. In the words of the former: Africa had "no history before the coming of Europeans" because "History only begins when men take to writing."[88] The latter, in a similar vein, construed African history only in relation to "the history of the Europeans in Africa." That "history of the Europeans in Africa" aside, there is only "the unrewarding gyrations of barbarous tribes in picturesque but irrelevant corners of the globe."[89] For Hegel, Newton, and Trevor-Roper, Africa "is no historical part of the world" because its inhabitants south of the Sahara could not be identified with these cultural benchmarks of civilization, among many other things: a belief system that emphasized monotheism, the invention and use of the wheel technology, alphabetism and literacy, the formation of centralized states, and the technology of building in stones.

In 1961 a lecturer in modern history at the University of Southampton, A.J. Hanna, had the following to say on the precolonial patterns of social organization in Africa while attempting to justify "European Rule in Africa."

> *Nevertheless "the partition of Africa" should not be thought to imply the destruction of any previously existing political unity or order in the African continent. There was none.* Most tribes were small, ranging in numbers from a few thousand to a few hundred thousand, and many tribes had no paramount chief or other bond of common loyalty and obedience, so that although they had the same language and customs they formed not one state but several—if the term 'state' may be applied at all to such conditions. Even the large powerful kingdoms, lorded over by their proud warrior-chiefs and in some cases administered by ingeniously elaborate hierarchies, can seldom have had more than about a million inhabitants, if as many. [My Emphasis][90]

For Hanna the formation of colonial states after the partition of Africa created political unity and order that never existed before. Colonial historiography as presented by Hanna, Newton, and Trevor-Roper, among many others, was ideologically driven to justify the conquest and colonization of Africa, including the imposition of the civilizing mission. The missionaries to West Africa, as the following excerpt culled from Bishop Samuel Crowther of the CMS Niger Mission indicates, endorsed and propagated that historiography and also justified the civilizing mission while proselytizing.

> The "Dark Continent" is properly applied to Africa. The inhabitants of a great portion of it are very *ignorant*, being *illiterate, unlettered, untaught*; all what they know is what was got by tradition from their forefathers, and handed down from generation to generation; they are therefore rude, barbarous, unmerciful, [and] superstitious.[91] [The emphasis is Crowther's]

Crowther, a Yoruba-speaking African by birth and an ex-slave, arguably represented those Africans who suffered from self-alienation and dislocation as a result of living (or attempting to live) in accordance with the socio-cultural prescriptions of the civilizing mission that disparaged black cognitive abilities and their moral characters. Crowther and his generation of African missionaries drawn from Sierra Leone, including the black West Indian missionaries who went to southern Nigeria between 1895 and 1925, were phenotypically black, but they did not identify themselves as culturally black. The sentiments of Crowther about Africa could substantiate the position of C.W. Mills when he argued that: "[T]here should be no essentialist illusions about anyone's intrinsic 'racial' virtue. All peoples can fall into Whiteness under the appropriate circumstances."[92] "'The term *functional Whites*,'" Rex Nettleford has also argued, not only "covers a range of skin-hues," but it "also refers to the cultural commitments such persons betray."[93] Along these lines of reasoning articulated by Mills and Nettleford, it could be argued that Crowther and the black West Indian missionaries to the Niger Mission were "'*functional Whites*.'"

For all of these related reasons, in *Cultural Change and Religious Conversion in West Africa,* John Kirby has argued that it would be more intellectually rewarding to evaluate and explain missionary proselytizing in Africa within the conceptual framework of "church-culture"—that is, European "church-culture." The concept of European church-culture is predicated on the assumptions of race and the civilizing mission; and it argues that:

> [A] new social order, a new political economy and a new culture must accompany the change to a new moral order. Proper European civilization was Christianity, and the only way to bring about conversion was to establish this cultural framework. [In the context of church-culture] what was Christian could, therefore, not abide with what was Africa.[94]

The commitment to this race-oriented church-culture agenda and philosophy accounted for the insistence of all missionary organizations on substituting Africa's indigenous socio-cultural and religious values with European values and practices. Missionary proselytizing, informed and influenced by this philosophy, constituted a veritable form of cultural invasion in Africa. In all forms of cultural invasion, according to Paulo Freire, "the invaders are the authors of, and actors in, the process; those they invade are moulded. The invaders choose; those they invade follow that choice—or are expected to follow it."[95] For cultural invasion to succeed, it is essential for the members of the group being invaded to perceive their reality from the perspective of the invaders—in this case, from the perspective of "whiteness." It was, in short, an attempt at conditioning the African to look at the African *self* from the standpoint of the values of "whiteness." This was how Steve Biko, the South African antiapartheid activist, articulated the theme of cultural invasion: "More than anyone else, the missionaries knew that not all they did was essential to the spread of the message. But the basic intention went much further than merely spreading the word. Their arrogance and their monopoly on truth, beauty, and moral judgment taught them to despise native customs and traditions and to seek to infuse their own new values into these [African] societies."[96]

The missionary and colonial school systems generally, and the Sunday school and boarding school systems in particular, constituted the most potent instruments for introducing and entrenching white normativity in African societies. The role of these schools was not simply to transmit the basic rudiments of literacy through subjects like reading, writing and arithmetic (the so-called "three Rs") for social functioning or existence. They were also intended to play a pivotal and critical role in the remolding of African children into *black Europeans* who will be proud to associate with the heritage and objectives of the imperial mother country—be it France or Britain. This is, for example, clearly reflected in the following excerpt taken from Bishop Johnson's *Journal Report* compiled in 1905 in southern Nigeria.

> The boarding school was in the early days of mission work in the Niger Delta a prominent feature because of the promise it gave and the hope it held out of being quickly very helpful in detaching the more youthful sections of the different communities from heathenism and its idolatry and winning them over to Christianity and through them influencing the different households which they severally represented.[97]

The situation was no different in the British Crown colony of Jamaica, as these comments from Geoff Palmer, an Afro-Jamaican beneficiary of the missionary school system, suggest.

> Reverend Nichols believed that reading was better
> than writing and arithmetic because reading
> enabled us to read the Bible. He also believed in
> what he called British order and contentment, so
> he made us form long queues round the Church
> and the School, and with vigorous conducting,
> taught us to sing songs in rounds, such as: 'Rule
> Britannia' (that strangely boastful song, written
> by the Scot, James Thomson during slavery), 'Row
> Boys Row,' 'O, my love's like a red rose,' (written
> by the great Scottish poet, Robert Burns, who
> applied to be a slave master in Jamaica).[98]

The primary aim of the Sunday school system, as an integral part of the missionary school system and the racially motivated civilizing mission, was for the ideological brainwashing of children during the most impressionable years of life. In pursuit of this aim, according to Karen F. Olwig, Sunday schools organized social events "designed to combat the evils of traditional festivals."[99] The various aspects of the training and orientation, given through the missionary boarding school and Sunday school systems, were designed to achieve the *true* or *genuine* conversion of all their pupils— that is, the total and complete socio-cultural transformation of their black personhood. In this condition of total alienation from their African socio-cultural heritage, the missionaries expected these pupils to embrace the British Empire and to uphold and regard Christian ideas as the ideal and pattern to be emulated.

Describing Africa as the "dark continent" and as "the land of childhood" reached its apogee, arguably, after the demise of Crowther in 1892. G.T. Basden, a member of the CMS Niger Mission, published *Among the Ibos of Nigeria* in 1921. Extending the trail blazed by Crowther, he argued thus: "[T]he Blackman does not himself know his own mind. He does the most extraordinary things and cannot explain why he does them. He is not controlled by logic; he is the victim of circumstance, and his policy is very largely one of drift."[100] After the publication of this book, according to the source just cited, Basden began to "gain recognition outside mission circles": "in 1925 he acquired a D. Litt"; and in 1930 "the colonial government [of Nigeria] asked him to become the representative of the Igbo people on the Legislative Council." This is a perfect illustration of the grand ideological alliance between the extraterritorial forces of change to foster the goals of the imperial mission in West Africa despite their subtle rhetorical differences, administrative styles and approaches on the so-called "native question." The evangelical objectives of missionaries were generally co-extensive with Europe's political and cultural perspectives on colonization in Africa; and, with equal zeal, many of them functioned as the political emissaries and representatives of European civilization in Africa while proselytizing.

The hamitic hypothesis and other race-oriented notions informing *Among the Ibos in Nigeria* got greatly elaborated in C.G. Seligman's *Races of Africa*,[101] first published in 1930. *Races of Africa*, drawing on a methodologically flawed linguistic classification that relied on a mixture of genetic, typological and anthropological criteria,[102] identified two white races in northern Africa: Hamites and Semites. In order to cast sub-Saharan Africa outside of the civilized world, by excluding it from history, Seligman declared:

> Apart from relatively Semitic influence—whether Phoenician [Carthaginian] and strictly limited, or Arabs [Muhammadan] and widely diffused—the civilizations of Africa are the civilizations of the Hamites, its history the record of these peoples and of their interaction with the two other African stocks, the Negro and the Bushman, whether this influence was exercised by civilized Egyptians or by such wider pastoralists as are represented at the present day by the Beja and the Somali.[103]

The implication of this passage is that the "non-white races" of Africa south of the Sahara, such as those peoples discussed by H.H. Simpson below, were uncivilized and also incapable of producing anything interesting because they did not make any contacts with the Hamites and/or the Semites, who belonged to "the same great branch of mankind as the whites,"[104] before the *second coming* of the Europeans in the later part of the nineteenth century. The hamitic hypothesis,[105] as it was called, influenced many missionary agents of the civilizing mission, including the black West Indian missionaries who went to Nigeria between 1895 and 1925. In the excerpt below, H.H. Simpson, a West Indian missionary in northern Nigeria, had ascribed Semitic origins to the Fulani-speaking people and also portrayed them as nomadic migrants to northern Nigeria from North Africa. Like Seligman, Simpson had also argued that the Nupe- and Hausa-speaking peoples in northern Nigeria were the beneficiaries of the civilizing influences of the Fulani-speaking people.

> It is very strange to say that this superior class of men [the Fulani] although they form the ruling class, yet they are a nomadic tribe of people who wander with their cattle.... These are supposed to be descendants of the Semitic people. Coming in from the North, ... they had to fight their way through the various tribes of North Africa and as they conquer tribe after tribe and bring them into subjection, these conquered tribes were compelled ... to give up their pagan ideas and accept the faith of Islam. They however did not stop to settle down but left enough of their body to rule and thus passed on. Now the Nupes and Hausas are greatly improved tribes not only by their Eastern civilization but by their inter-marriage with these Fulani people.[106]

The essence of the arguments by Seligman and Simpson is that the nineteenth and twentieth century European civilizing missions to sub-Saharan Africa represented an unfinished agenda of the Hamites and Semites. These arguments taken together, which portrayed black Africa as incapable of producing anything interesting until the arrival of persons from "white Africa," represented an excellent example of racial norming: "You are what you are in part because you originate from a certain kind of space, and that space has [certain] properties in part because it is inhabited by creatures like yourself."[107] The flawed concept of racial norming, as this passage culled from the "Geographical Basis of World History" by Hegel illustrates, is predicated on the idea of geographical determinism in the evolution of human societies, institutions and civilizations.

> In terms of world history, the natural conditions in Africa are on the whole negative; but in Asia, they are positive. This also explains why the Asians have so great an appreciation of nature. Just as nature is the basis of history itself, so also must it be the basis of our study of history. The natural world and the spiritual world together form the living totality of history.[108]

In the same essay, Hegel also argued that Africa's "isolation [from world history] is not just a result of its tropical nature, but an essential consequence of its geographical character."[109] This was, in sum, the basis of nineteenth century race thinking: nature and geography were responsible for the cultural differences and achievement gaps between Europeans and Africans. Let me put it slightly differently and sarcastically: nature and geography, having conspired, are to be blamed for the moral depravity, savagery and barbarism associated with Africa and African personhood. This was what Basden probably meant when he said that: the Blackman "is a victim of circumstance." The aim of the civilizing mission—seen at least from the humanitarian standpoint of its European and African protagonists—was to minimize or eliminate the perceived cultural differences through the Christianization and colonization of the continent. The civilizing effort, seen from this perspective, was a rescue and/or redemption mission. The excerpt below, culled from Hanna's "European Rule in Africa," represents that perspective substantially.

> In the broadest perspective of history it was out of the question that Africa could continue forever in economic stagnation and political chaos, ravaged in the west by fanatical Moslem conquerors, in the east by tribes who were armed and paid by Arab slave traders, and in the south by the predatory hordes who had spread northwards from Zululand, while in every other continent the facility of communications and the pace of economic development were rapidly increasing. *Yet it is virtually certain that conditions in Africa would still be roughly what they were a century ago, had it not been for the introduction of European administration, European instruction, and the contact with the European economy.* It is true that, in West Africa if not in other parts of the continent, the African had already given expression to considerable creative powers, in sculpture and other handicrafts which were sometimes of outstanding quality. But there was no technological progress, no stirring of the spirit of inquiry, no questioning of the time-hallowed customs of the tribe. [My Emphasis][110]

Because it was also believed, as the foregoing comments indicate, that "In Africa proper man has not progressed beyond a merely sensuous existence, and has found it absolutely impossible to develop any further"[111] without the assistance of Europeans and Asians, the hamitic hypothesis developed into a sweeping racial system of explanation that dealt with any noteworthy forms of cultural achievements found in the continent during the colonial period. Euro-centric historians of southern Africa, for example, invented Asian and Portuguese origins for the famous stone ruins of the Mwene Mutapa Empire or the Great Zimbabwe.[112] Ultimately the hamitic hypothesis was also aimed at impressing on Africans that they have been made into history by the descendants of the white race—the real makers of history—in order to legitimate and stabilize the unequal power relationships between Africans and Europeans during the colonial period.

Let me summarize, at this stage, what I have been trying to say above in the words of Robert G. Armstrong, a student of socio-linguistics and one of the most ardent critics of the hamitic hypothesis:

> The great majority of the Europeans who came to Africa accepted it as axiomatic that the Negro peoples were incapable of inventing or producing anything interesting, subtle, or complex. When, therefore, interesting, subtle and complex things were found in such places as West Africa (or for that matter Uganda or Rwanda-Burundi or Southern Rhodesia (Zimbabwe), the problem of 'science' was to discover from what place outside of Negro Africa it had come and what 'white' people had brought it there.[113]

This condensed critique of knowledge production tells us how and why Africa came to be known and called the "Dark Continent" down the centuries; and it also tells us why its inhabitants were perceived as benighted subpersons by their European conquerors and overlords during the latter part of the nineteenth and early twentieth century.

The questions we ask and the narratives we construct on the basis of the "evidence" or "facts" available to us, whether as natural scientists, social scientists, or historians, will invariably depend on our intellectual worldview. Put differently: our worldview will not only determine how and why we construct narratives, but it will also determine what we consider as objects worthy of scientific or historical investigation. Agents of race and the civilizing mission, influenced by these two interlocking ideologies, wittingly or unwittingly, created an essentialized black African group identity between the nineteenth and the first four decades of the twentieth century. That image, in varying degrees, has survived in Africa, Britain, the West Indies, and the United States of America.

Blackness for all those seeking to enthrone whiteness signified or symbolized the lack of culture, not cultural difference with Europeans. Elizabethan Englishmen, according to W.D. Jordan, "found in the idea of blackness a way of expressing some of their most engrained values." Seen through their own eyes, for example, "White and black connoted purity and filthiness, virginity and sin, virtue and baseness, beauty and ugliness, beneficence and evil, God and the devil."[114] Here is yet another dramatic over valuation and valorization of European selfhood drawn to devalue and demean African personhood: "The European is vehement, energetic, proud, tenacious and revengeful, [while] the African is docile, gentle, humble, grateful, and commonly forgiving. The one is ambitious and easily aroused; the other is meek, easily contented, and easily subdued. The one is to the other as the willow is to the oak."[115] In addition to perceiving Africans as being in urgent need of European paternalism because they were childlike, stupid, and lazy, they were at other times portrayed as deserving containment and subjugation because of being vicious, wild, explosive, impulsive and irrational. These examples clearly illustrate what was said at the beginning: The European "process of forming the notion of a geopolitical self is … symbiotically linked to the negation of that self; that is … the process of determining 'what' constitutes Europe and things European requires formulating what does not constitute such phenomenon."

Europe, to a certain extent, *created* a discourse about Africa as a primitive continent in part to exalt its own sense of *self*. Race and the civilizing mission, in this philosophical, cultural and political endeavor, largely influenced the use and/or misuse of "evidence" in those narratives that defined and constructed blackness and African personhood in the period leading up to colonization. These interlocking concepts, in large part, also provided the ideological basis for the establishment of those European colonial administrative systems—be it the system of *Assimilation* and *Association* as identified in Francophone territories, or the system of *Indirect Rule* as identified in Anglophone territories—that were designed to facilitate the economic exploitation of African societies during the period leading up to independence. Given these facts it became necessary and imperative, during the decolonization process, to philosophically challenge and interrogate these interlocking concepts of race and civilizing mission in order to undermine the legitimacy, basis and structure of colonial rule in Africa.

PART FOUR

Concluding Comments: Combating European Constructions of Blackness and African Personhood—the Contributions of "The New African Historiography" after Independence

Many educated Africans, especially those beneficiaries of the missionary and colonial educational systems earlier mentioned and discussed, suffered from self-alienation and psychological dislocation as a result of the intense verbal and written ideological assaults unleashed against blackness and African personhood. Self-alienation, ideological brainwashing, and psychological disorientation, from James Ngugi's standpoint, were very well vividly demonstrated by those elites:

> Who took on the [European] tongue and adopted
> the style of the conquerors. They it was who har-
> kened to the voice of the missionary God, cried
> halleluyah, and raised their eyes to heaven. They
> derided the old gods and recoiled with studied or
> genuinely acquired horror from the primitive rites
> of their people.[116]

One consequence of self-alienation and psychological disorientation, as the excerpt indicates, is the development
of an idolatrous worship and apish imitation of European things, mannerisms, and symbols. In that situation European languages and symbolisms, etiquettes and mannerisms, for example, easily became the standard for assessing
elegance in speech and acceptable public behavior, while
their dresses, and modes of dressing, similarly became the
hallmarks of beautiful and good fashions. Generally, owing
to the connection the civilizing mission established in the
minds of many black consumers between consumption and
civilization, European manufactures are often preferred to
indigenous ones in Africa. The unhealthy practice of "skin
bleaching" found among some black people in Africa and
the New World African diaspora, furthermore, is traceable
to one source: the banal and profane thinking that the European skin colour is aesthetically more graceful and attractive
than theirs. Many black people have accepted in the deepest
recesses of their minds that black is in fact inferior to white.
This is the most pernicious effect of colonialism and the civilizing mission on black psychology and personhood globally.

In 1961 Leopold Sedar Senghor of Senegal, an exponent
of the Negritude Philosophy, also articulated the adverse
impact of race and the civilizing mission on educated African
elites in French-speaking Africa in these words:

> With docility we accepted the values of the West,
> its discursive reason and its techniques. Our
> ambition was to become photographic negatives

of the colonizers: "black-skinned Frenchmen." It went even further, for we would have blushed, if we could have blushed, about our black skin, our frizzled hair, our flat noses, above all for the values of our traditional civilization.... Our people ... secretly, caused us shame.[117]

Ironically, notwithstanding the seemingly very profound acculturation of those educated and Christianized "black-skinned Europeans," as dramatically highlighted by Senghor and Ngugi, they were still being contemptuously perceived and described disdainfully as "humorous caricatures of 'civilized' men" by some European critics and commentators on the West Coast of Africa.[118] Neither thoroughly white nor black culturally, their *liminal* situation or status could arguably be compared with the plight of the "marginal man" as portrayed by R.E. Park: "[O]ne who lives in two worlds, in both of which he is more or less a stranger."[119]

In recognition of these awful existential conditions and their philosophical implications for individual and national postcolonial identity construction, African anti-colonial activists and publicists, in concert with intellectuals drawn from the universities, engendered the "Historiography of Self-Assertion"—also known and called "The New African Historiography." The "Historiography of Self-Assertion," to put it in the words of C.W. Mills, unreservedly endorsed the following political agenda, among other intellectual and scholastic objectives: "The exposure of the misrepresentations of Eurocentrism, not-so-innocent 'white lies' and 'white mythologies'"[120] in order to promote blackness and the Negro African personhood. Arguably, "The New African Historiography," as an act of epistemic resistance, was also about postcolonial identity politics and identity construction and/or reconstruction.

The ideals or utopias of Pan Africanism, Negritude, Black Consciousness, and the African Personality, informed the epistemic resistance that characterized this new form of historical writing and race thinking; and it was intended to create a sense of self worth, dignity, and solidarity among the peoples of Africa and their leaders, including the peoples of African descent in the New World. Africa and its leaders, after the dehumanizing experiences of alien European rule in the continent, were attempting to reassert and rediscover themselves through the medium of "The New African Historiography." All of these utopias and/or concepts were, in varying degrees, driven and influenced by a sense of race belonging, the desire for cultural affirmation and/or reaffirmation, history, politics, and geography. These factors, it is important to reiterate, also informed the European imperial narratives being challenged by these anti-colonial intellectuals, publicists and activists. Put differently, these intellectuals, like their European oppressors, were acknowledging race as the basis for promoting African nationalism and solidarity.

Pan-Africanists, it has been said, "looked forward to a dispensation whereby Africans [and persons of African descent in the New World] would redeem themselves from a world system that largely marginalized them because of their skin pigmentation."[121] Negritude, in the words of one of its greatest exponents, Senghor: "[I]s the awareness by a particular social group of people of its own situation in the world, and the expression of it by means of a concrete image."[122] Alongside Negritude, which was more popular among the educated elites in French-speaking African countries, was the notion of African Personality articulated by Nkrumah among English-speaking African countries. According to E. Mphahlele, in *The African Image*, "the ideology is really a search for ... the truth about [the African self]."[123]

Inherent in these ideas or utopias is the notion of an essentialized group black identity and consciousness. This, for example, is how Steve B. Biko, the antiapartheid activist of South Africa, presented the idea of Black Consciousness referred to earlier:

> Black Consciousness is an attitude of mind and
> a way of life, the most positive call to emanate
> from the black world for a long time. *Its essence is*
> *the realization by the black man of the need to rally*
> *together with his brothers around the cause of their*
> *oppression*—the blackness of their skin—and to
> operate as a group to rid themselves of the shack-
> les that bind them to perpetual servitude.[124] [My
> emphasis]

Founded on the essentialist notion of "race," Black Consciousness advocated for "group pride and the determination
of the black [race] to rise and attain the envisaged self."[125]
For the advocates of these ideologies—Black Consciousness,
Pan Africanism, Negritude, and the African Personality—
"race" and "blackness" (like "race" and "whiteness" for Europeans) were generally perceived and pursued as the sound
and effective foundations for determining and constructing
social identities and policies, cultural affiliations, and political movements.

In consonance with these ideas, the new historiography
was expected to "[provide] the impetus for Africans to find
pride in their past achievements in all spheres of life";[126] and
its practitioners had to demonstrate the "African Initiatives"
in history in order to refute the idea that Africans never contributed to the growth and development of human civilizations. George Lamming, a West Indian writer and activist,
articulated the same value that the new historiography of
self-assertion was attempting to promote in Africa in these
words.

> If a people are shaped by the view that they are
> made into history by some chosen few who are
> the real makers of history, you stabilize the rela-
> tion of dominant and dominated…. If we could
> ever succeed in planting in people, not only the
> idea, but the fact, in their consciousness, that they

are the makers of history, then you alter the relationship between them and those who hold them
in their hands.[127]

In the late 1950s and early 1960s—the decade of Africa's
independence—reputable schools of history emerged in
the following African universities to pursue and promote
this new endeavor and consciousness: the Ibadan University nationalist school of historiography under K.O. Dike,
J.C. Anene, S.O. Biobaku, E.A. Ayandele, and J.A. Ajayi, in
Nigeria; the Cheikh Anta Diop school based at the University of Senegal in Senegal; the University of Nairobi school
under the aegis of Bethwell Alan Ogot in Kenya; and the
Dar es Salem school under Terence Ranger in Tanzania.

This new African historiography, it has been widely
accepted, was led and championed by the late Kenneth
Onwuka Dike and the aforementioned generation of trained
historians scattered across the continent. In the words of
Afigbo, one of the former students of Dike:

> Professor Dike, 1917-1983, is remembered as a
> distinguished scholar, a consummate educational
> administrator and a statesman. In the field of
> scholarship, Prof. Dike is recognized across the
> world as the father of modern African history. *It*
> *was Professor Dike who changed the world's percep-*
> *tion of the history of the peoples of Africa,* introduced
> the modalities and set up the appropriate struc-
> tures for the study, teaching and general dissemi-
> nation of African history.[128] [My emphasis]

Like Dike, Ogot "functioned as pioneer and midwife of the
[new] historical writing and publication in Kenya and the
East African region"; and his history of the Luo-speaking
peoples, like Dike's account of trade and politics in the Niger
Delta, was well received as an "epoch-making feat in the heart
of imperial London where he had studied."[129] "The New

Historiography," according to Afigbo, was "able to establish beyond doubt (reasonable or unreasonable) that there is an African past; that it is knowable; and that among the basic ingredients of this past were the migrations of peoples, the rise and fall of empires, the economic, political and cultural interaction of peoples not only within the continent but also between the peoples of the continent and those of Arabia, India, China and Europe."[130]

Notwithstanding their individual international alliances with the competing capitalist and socialist blocs during the era of the Cold War, this new form of historical writing was well received and perceived by all the freedom fighters in the continent during the 1960s—for example, Nnamdi Azikiwe of Nigeria, Julius Nyerere of Tanzania, Jomo Kenyatta of Kenya, Leopold Sedar Senghor of Senegal, Patrice Lumumba of Congo, and Kwame Nkrumah of Ghana—as the ideological wing of the anti-colonial campaigns. These comments from Lumumba are very instructive and revealing because they corroborate the fact that African nationalists had sought for a useable past during the anti-colonial struggles; and they had actually looked up to African academic historians to play a critical and decisive role in the construction and provision of that useable past.

> History will have its say one day—not the history they [imperialists] teach in Brussels, Paris, Washington or the United Nations, but the history taught in the countries set free from colonialism and its puppet rulers. Africa will write her own history, and both north and south of the Sahara it will be a history of glory and dignity.[131]

It appears that there was equally, from the outset, an awareness among the university intellectuals pioneering the "Historiography of Self-Assertion" that a rich historical and cultural past (real or invented) was going to be needed for the postcolonial exercise of identity construction or reconstruction, cultural affirmation or reaffirmation, and nation building, in the continent generally. It is said, for example, that Dike collaborated willingly and readily with these nationalists, particularly Azikiwe, Nkrumah, Kenyatta, and Senghor, to promote the construction of a befitting and useable African personhood after the attainment of independence.[132] Emphasizing the relevance of the new historiography to Africa's quest for independence and nation buiding, Ogot also pointed out that: "political independence could only have meaning if it was accompanied by historical independence."[133]

Jomo Kenyatta also argued in *Facing Mount Kenya* thus: [I]t is ... culture ... that gives a man his human dignity as well as his material prosperity. It teaches him mental and moral values and makes him feel it worthwhile to work and fight for liberty."[134] What Kenyatta was articulating in effect, which appears to be very much in synch with those ideas associated with Lumumba and George Lamming above, is that a continent deprived of its history and culture cannot create or recreate a decent and worthy self-image for its inhabitants. One of the aims of "The New Historiography," in essence, was ideological: To create an African-centered world—that is, the centering of "blackness," as opposed to "whiteness"—as the perspective on and of reality, in order to produce some usable knowledge about the past that would help nurture and nourish a new African personhood after colonialism.

In redefining and representing blackness in consonance with the political agenda of the "Historiography of Self-Assertion," which specifically sought to explain African achievements in the context of other world civilizations, Chiekh Anta Diop and Chancellor Williams have argued that the ancient Egyptian civilization was the achievement of black populations (not white Africans). In the words of Williams: "The land of the Blacks was not only the 'cradle of civilization' itself but that the blacks were once the leading people on earth; that Egypt once was not only all blacks, but the very name 'Egypt' was derived from the Blacks; and that the blacks were the pioneers in the sciences, medicine, architecture, writing, and were the first builders in stone, etc."[135] Regarding Diop, Alagoa has observed that: "While still a student in Paris, [he] had espoused the doctrine of the black origins of Egyptian, and therefore, of Greek, and Western civilization, a position he defended in research, writing and public lectures and symposia through Africa, the Caribbean, the Americas, and Europe."[136]

One of the aims of Diop, like Dike and Ogot, "was to bracket the colonial experience as simply a moment in the long history of Africa."[137] Owing to these views, according to *Presence Africane,* Diop has been perceived by the West as a "heretic," "anathema," and "a paranoid Black"; while being seen and applauded as "a protector standing guard at the gate" of "the black man's identity" by Africans.[138] The "restorative" projects of Chancellor Williams and Cheikh Anta Diop, according to N. Akbar, "has expanded and intensified the significant work that was begun by W.E.B. DuBois, J.A. Rogers, Carter G. Woodson, Martin Delaney, George G.M. James, and hundreds of others who realized the significance of reviving the history and telling the story of African accomplishment as a significant part of the Black liberation process."[139]

The description and perception of Diop as a "restorer," "a liberator," and "a protector standing guard at the gate" of "the black man's identity," for example, could underscore the point made by Ochwada when he argued that: although "The New Historiography" was ideologically driven to facilitate "the struggle for independence," its practitioners also "wanted knowledge that was useful for *enhancing their position in society.*"[My emphasis][140] Let us also recall that, notwithstanding their education and Westernization, it was not uncommon for European commentators to disdainfully perceive and describe them as "humorous caricatures of 'civilized' men." Bearing all of this in mind it might then be safe to argue that, even at the individual level, Africa's postcolonial intellectuals and political leaders were indeed engaged in the politics of identity construction. Sadiq Rashid has, in fact, described the mid-twentieth century (1950-1970s) relationship between the academic community and the political leaders of Africa in the following way.

> [It was] a period of mutual tolerance and amicable cooperation between the academic community and the policy making entities and of mutual accommodation and willful cooperation when views of academicians were solicited by the latter, *while the former readily obliged and often take pride in being associated with the honour of contributing to the crafting of national policies and exposure to the limelight as a result thereof.*[141] [My emphasis]

"How you construct identity," K. Thomas has argued, "is predicated on how you construct desire: desire for recognition; quest for visibility; the sense of being acknowledged; [and] a deep desire for association."[142] Given these comments on "how and why you construct identity," including the earlier comments of Ochwada (a critic of the new historiography) and Rashid, it could be argued that the production of an idealized and unproblematized African past was in part also propelled by the quest for personal and group recognition, visibility, acknowledgement, and association in the wider world.

The various forms of ideologically driven historical writings considered in this essay—the "Historiography of Self-Assertion" that sought to forge a new African personhood on the basis of an idealized and unproblematized past, including the European constructions of whiteness and blackness through the agents of race and the civilizing mission intended to enhance the colonial subjugation of Africa—have collectively substantiated and underscored the following three key theoretical points pertaining to the politics of identity formation as articulated by A.K. Appiah. First, "Identities are complex and multiple and grow out of a history of changing responses to economic, political, and cultural forces, almost always in opposition to other identities." Second, "Identities flourish despite ... our 'misrecognition' of their origins; despite, that is, their roots in myths and in lies." In addition to what has been said in the essay, this point was also very pellucidly demonstrated in the just concluded American presidential elections: certain segments of the electorate deliberately tried to devalue Barack Obama's personhood and candidacy because of his black identity. That attempt, including the attempt to portray him as an Arab, could also corroborate Appiah's final characterization: "There is no large place for reason [objectivism] in the construction—as opposed to the study and management—of identities."[143] Obama's election victory, arguably, rested in part on effective identity management as he negotiated for support among segments of the multi-cultural voting populations in the United States.

Finally, for this study that has explored the global tensions between "whiteness" and "blackness," it may be considered befitting to make the following interrelated and overlapping comments regarding the global significance of Obama's historic victory. The civil rights laws enacted under the Lyndon Johnson administration in the 1960s, it is pertinent to note, had brought African-Americans some measure of equality with regard to voting rights and, to a much lesser degree, school segregation. In other areas, however, African-Americans continued to suffer immense discrimination on the basis of color. In this context Obama's electoral victory, arguably, could be described as a global symbol of victory against racism. It could also be described as symbolizing the climax of the positive changes taking place in the global perception of "blackness" since the attainment of Africa's independence from colonial rule and the philosophical triumph of the Civil Rights Movement against racism in the United States after decades of bitter and bloody struggles.[144]

As a result of these changes before the presidential elections, it appears that more than ever before there are now more white people willing to engage in open public political conversations without being overly prejudiced by the age-old white group thinking about "blackness." It also appears that these persons, in addition to showing more willingness to respect the liberal democratic values of black individual autonomy and personhood, are also less prepared to support political movements that are built around the racial identity of "whiteness." To fully appreciate the philosophical significance of the political behaviour of the white American voters, the following insightful sentiments of Ngugi on identity construction may be worth recalling.

> [How] we view ourselves, our own environment even, is very much dependent on where we stand in relationship to imperialism in its colonial and neo-colonial stages; *that if we are to do anything about our individual and collective being today, then we have to coldly and consciously look at what imperialism (and race) have been doing to our view of ourselves in the universe.* [My emphasis][145]

My overall point here, which is intended to reinforce the preceding closing argument, is as follows: Obama won in part because, within the United States of America, many more white persons have started taking a cold and conscious look "at what imperialism (and race) have been doing to our view of ourselves in the universe." All of these points when taken together could, arguably, also indicate the imminent bankruptcy awaiting those cultural and social organizations that still articulate identity-based programmes, including national and global political movements predicated on the essentialist concept of race.

Notes

1. L.R. Gordon, *Disciplinary Decadence: Living Thought in Trying Times* (London: Paradigm Publishers 2006), 29.

2. Quoted from R.G. Collingwood, *The Idea of History* (Originally published in 1946. Reprint, Oxford: Oxford University Press, 1978) 59.

3. Quoted from E.J. Alagoa, *The Practice of History in Africa* (Port Harcourt: Onyoma Research Publications, 2007) 123.

4. Cited from T. Mkandawire, "Introduction" in *African Intellectuals: Rethinking Politics, Language, and Development* ed. T. Mkandawire. (London: Zed Books, 2005) 3-4.

5. Ibid., 6.

6. E.J. Alagoa, *The Python's Eye: The Past in the Living Present* (Port Harcourt: Harrison Publication Company, 1977) 19 [University of Port Harcourt Inaugural Lecture].

7. K. A. Appiah, *In My Father's House: Africa in the Philosophy of Culture* (Oxford: Oxford Univ. Press, 1992) 178.

8. A.E. Afigbo, *The Poverty of African Historiography* (Lagos: Afrografika Publishers, 1977) 2-3.

9. E.B. Rugemer, *The Problem of Emancipation: The Caribbean Roots of the American Civil War* (Baton Rouge: Louisiana State Univ. Press 2008) p228.

10. Ibid, 192.

11. Ibid, 2.

12. Ibid, 228.

13. T. Shelby, *We Who are Dark*: *The Philosophical Foundations of Black Solidarity* (Cambridge, Massachusetts: The Belknap Press of the Harvard Univ. Press, 2005) 2.

14. G.O.M. Tasie, *Christian Missionary Enterprise in the Niger Delta, 1864-1918* (Leiden: E.J. Brill, 1978) 133.

15. D.M. Schreuder, "The Cultural Factor in Victorian Imperialism: a case-study of the British 'civilizing mission'" in *The*

Journal of Imperial and Commonwealth History, IV, no. 3 (May 1967) 283-317.

16. P.D. Curtin, *The Image of Africa: British Ideas and Action, 1780-1850* (Madison: The University of Wisconsin Press 1964).

17. N. Akbar, *Breaking the Chains of Psychological Slavery* (Tallahassee, FL: Mind Productions &Associates 1996) 34.

18. Gordon, *Disciplinary Decadence*, 64.

19. W. Wariboko, *Ruined by "Race": Afro-Caribbean Missionaries and the Evangelization of Southern Nigeria, 1895-1925* (Trenton, NJ: Africa World Press, 2007) 9.

20. E.B. Rugemer, *The Problem of Emancipation* 33-41.

21. Quoted from R.W. West, *Brazza of the Congo: Exploration and Exploitation in Equatorial Africa* (London: Redwood Press, 1973) 23.

22. W.A.J. Okumu, *The African Renaissance: History, Significance and Strategy* (Trenton, NJ: Africa World Press, 2002) 41.

23. C.W. Mills, *The Racial Contract* (Ithaca, NY: Cornell Univ. Press, 1997) 21.

24. P. Gilroy, *Against Race: Imagining Political Culture beyond the Color Line* (Cambridge: Cambridge Univ. Press 2000) 57.

25. Gordon, *Disciplinary Decadence*, 71.

26. K. Malik, *The Meaning of Race: Race, History and Culture in Western Society* (London: MacMillan Press, 1996) 45.

27. Gordon, *Disciplinary Decadence*, 68.

28. Malik, *The Meaning of Race*, 40.

29. E.C. Eze, *Race and the Enlightenment: A Reader* (Oxford: Blackwell 1997) 4.

30. Malik, *The Meaning of Race*, 83.

31. Gordon, *Disciplinary Decadence*, 70.

32. Malik, *The Meaning of Race*, 150-156.

33. T. Ranger, "The Invention of Tradition in Colonial Africa," in *Perspectives on Africa* ed. R.R. Grinker and C.B. Steiner (Oxford: Blackwell, 1997) 600.

34. J.N. Cheetham, "First Impressions of West Africa: Onitsha and its Neighbourhood," *Southport Visitor*, 27 January 1900; for more on this see: Wariboko, *Ruined by "Race,"* 112.

35. S. Bessis, *Western Supremacy: The Triumph of an Idea?* (New York: Zed Books, 2001) 41.

36. W.E. Wariboko, "James Norris Cheethan and the CMS Civilizing Mission to Igboland: An Examination of His Letters to the *Southport Visitor*, 1899-1931" *The Nigerian Academic Forum* Vol. 6, no. 3 (April, 2004) 15-30.

37. D. Fraser, *The Future of Africa.* (London: Young People's Missionary Movement, 1911. Reprint, Westport, CT: Negro University Press, 1970) 10.

38. Phillip, *The Image of Africa*, 63.

39. T. J. Barron, "James Stephen, the 'Black Race' and British Colonial Administration, 1813-47" *The Journal of Imperial and Commonwealth History*, V, no. 2 (January 1977) 146.

40. Curtin, *The Image of Africa*, 257.

41. Bessis, *Western Supremacy*, 40.

42. Curtin, *The Image of Africa*, 406.

43. Ernest Renan, *Oeuvre Completes* (Cited in Bessis, *Western Imperialism*, 2001) 26.

44. D.M. Schreuder, "The Cultural Factor in Victorian Imperialism" *Journal of Imperial and Commonwealth History*, IV, no. 3 (May 1976) 283-317.

45. K. Pearson, *National Life from the Standpoint of Science* (Cited in Bessis, *Western Supremacy*) 33.

46. G.W.F. Hegel, "The Geographical Basis of World History" in *Race and the Enlightenment*, ed. E.C. Eze. (Oxford: Blackwell 1997) 117.

47. Jules Ferry, "Speech to the Chamber of Deputies," 28 July 1885 (Cited in Bessis, *Western Supremacy*) 26.

48. Regence de Tunis, Protectorate Francaise, "Direction de l'Agriculture, du commerce et de la colonization," (Cited in Bessis, *Western Supremacy*) 39.

49. Mills, *The Racial Contract*, 11.

50. Rugemer, *The Problem of Emancipation* 263.

51. Schreuder, "The Cultural Factor in Victorian Imperialism" 283.

52. M. Crowther, "The Impact of Colonialism" in *The African Experience Volume 1: Essays* ed. J.N. Paden & E.W. Soja. (Evanston: Northwestern University Press, 1970) 238.

53. Bessis, *Western Supremacy*, 39.

54. T. Ballantyne, "Empire, Knowledge and Culture: From Proto-Globalization to Modern Globalization" in *Globalization in World History* ed. A.G. Hopkins. (London: Pimilco, 2002) 132.

55. Malik, *The Meaning of Race*, 118.

56. *The Times*, 12 September 1910 (Cited in Malik, *The Meaning of Race*) 118.

57. H. Deegan, *The Politics of the New South Africa: Apartheid and After* (New York: Longman, 2001) 4.

58. A. Conway, *The History of the Negro in the United States* (London: The Historical Association, 1968) 17.

59. Enoch Powell, "Speech at Eastbourne" 16 November 1968 (Cited in Malik, *The Meaning of Race*) 143.

60. G.H. Palmer, *The Enlightenment Abolished: Citizens of Britishness* (Midlothian, Scotland: Henry Publishing, 2007) 69.

61. Palmer, *The Enlightenment Abolished*, 58.

62. Mills, *The Racial Contract*, 56.

63. Hegel, "Geographical Basis of World History" in *Race and the Enlightenment*, 127.

64. P. Sherlock, *Jamaica's Proud Heritage* (Undated monograph published by the Office of the Vice Chancellor, Mona

Campus, the University of the West Indies, and endorsed by the National Council on Education, Jamaica) 23.

65. Bessis, *Western Supremacy*, 11.

66. Ibid., 40.

67. G3A3/1917/12 Sidney Smith to G.T. Manley, 10 August 1917.

68. K.A. Appiah, "Race, Culture, and Identity: Misunderstood Connections," in *Colour Consciousness: The Political Morality of Race* ed. K.A. Appiah and A. Gutman (Princeton, NJ: Princeton Univ. Press, 1996) 82.

69. G3A3/1914/13, Sidney Smith to G.T. Manley, 3 January 1914.

70. C.W. Mills, *Blackness Visible: Essays on Philosophy and Race* (London: Cornell University Press, 1998) 127.

71. Gilroy, *Against Race*, 57.

72. Curtin, *The Image of Africa*, 432.

73. Jean Suret-Canale, "Centenaire de la Conference de Berlin" in *Documents of the International Colloquium held in Brazaville, April 1985*. (Paris: Presence Africaine 1987).

74. Curtin, *The Image of Africa*, 261.

75. J.N. Cheetham, "Southern Nigeria- Missionaries and the Denationalization of the Negro," *Southport Visitor* 23-March—1912.

76. *Mr. Chamberlain's Speeches*, 2 vols. ed. Charles W. Boyd. London: Constable 1914 (Cited in Bessis, *Western Supremacy*) 37.

77. J.N. Cheetham, "Southern Nigeria—The Future of the Country," *Southport Visitor* 4 May 1913.

78. Ballantyne, "Empire, Knowledge and Culture," 31.

79. Eze, *Race and the Enlightenment*, 5.

80. Reverend W.T. Mumford, "A Special Appeal to the Women and Girls of Jamaica," *Jamaica Diocesan Magazine* no 1, (August 1932); also cited in W. Wariboko, "West Indian Church in

West Africa: The Pongas Mission among the Susus and Its Portrayal of Blackness, 1851-1935" in *Missions, States, and European Expansion in Africa*. ed. C.J. Korieh and R.C. Njoku. (London: Routledge 2007) 35-52 .

81. Curtin, *The Image of Africa*, 324.

82. Eze, *Race and the Enlightenment*, 7.

83. "The Missionary Exhibition," *Jamaica Times* 7 May 1910.

84. M. Conway, *Travels in South Kensington* (Cited in Ballantyne, "Empire, Knowledge and Culture") 123.

85. E.J. Alagoa, *The Practice of History in Africa: A History of African Historiography* (Port Harcourt, Nigeria: Onyoma Research Publications, 2007) 124-125.

86. Ibid., 125.

87. G.W.F. Hegel, *The Philosophy of History* (New York: Dover Publications, 1956) 99.

88. A.P. Newton, "Africa and Historical Research" *Journal of the African Society* 22, (1922-3).

89. H. Trevor-Roper, "The Rise of Christian Europe" *The Listener* (28 November 1963) 871.

90. A.J. Hannah, "European Rule in Africa" *Journal of The Historical Association* No 46 (1961) 13.

91. G3A3/1890/140, "Difficulties on the way of Missionary Work on the West Coast of Africa," August 1890; also see: W.E. Wariboko, *Planting Church Culture in New Calabar: Some Neglected Aspects of Missionary Enterprise in the Eastern Niger Delta, 1865-1918* (Bethesda, MD: International Scholars Publications, 1998) 11.

92. Mills, *The Racial Contract*, 128-129.

93. R.M. Nettleford, *Mirror Mirror: Identity, Race and Protest in Jamaica* (Kingston: LMH Publishing Limited, 1998) xxxiv.

94. J.P. Kirby, "Cultural Change and Religious Conversion in West Africa," in *Religions in Africa*. eds. D.T. Blakely, E.A.W. Beek, & D.L. Thomson. (London: Heinemann, 1994) 61.

95. P. Freire, *Pedagogy of the Oppressed* (Penguin: England, 1990) 46 [Translated by Myra Bergman Ramos].

96. S.B. Biko, "Black Consciousness and the Quest for a True Humanity" in *The African Philosophical Reader* ed. P.H. Coetzee and A.P.J. Roux. (London: Routledge, 2003) 83.

97. G3A3/1906/168 Bishop J. Johnson, "Journal Report" December- July, 1905.

98. Palmer, *The Enlightenment Abolished*, 64.

99. K.F. Olwig, *Global Culture, Island Identity: Continuity and Change in the Afro-Caribbean Community of Nevis* (Switzerland: Harwood Academic Publishers, 1993) 90.

100. D.V.D. Bersselaar, "Missionary Knowledge and the State in Colonial Nigeria: On How G.T. Basden Became an Expert" *History in Africa* 33 (2006) 437.

101. C.G. Seligman, *Races of Africa* (Oxford: Oxford University Press) 1966.

102. R.J. Hayward, "AfroAsiatic" in *African Languages: An Introduction*. ed. B. Heine and D. Nurse. (Cambridge: Cambridge Univ. Press, 2000) 74-98.

103. Seligman, *Races of Africa*, 61.

104. Ibid., 61.

105. E.R. Sanders, "The Hamitic Hypothesis: Its origins and functions in Time Perspective," *Journal of African History* Vol. 10, no 4, (1969) 521-32.

106. H.H. Simpson, "Nigeria—the Land of the Near Future [part two]" *Jamaica Times,* 16 October 1915; see the full discussion on Simpson in Wariboko, *Ruined by "Race"* 199-203.

107. Mills, *The Racial Contract*, 42.

108. Eze, *Race and the Enlightenment*, 143.

109. Ibid., 124.

110. Hanna, "European Rule in Africa" 11.

111. Ibid., 122.

112. J.J. Williams, *Hebrewisms of West Africa* (New York: The Dial Press, 1930) 173-174 (The entire narrative of this text is informed by the race assumptions of the Hamitic hypothesis).

113. R.G. Armstrong, *The Study of West African Languages* (Ibadan: Ibadan Univ. Press 1967) 3-4 (This text is an expanded version of an inaugural lecture delivered at the University of Ibadan on 20 February 1964).

114. W.D. Jordan, *The White Man's Burden: Historical Origins of Racism in the United States* (Oxford: Oxford Univ. Press, 1974) 6.

115. Cited in Curtin, *The Image of Africa*, 27.

116. J. Ngugi, "The Independence of Africa and Cultural Decolonization" *UNESCO Courier* (January 1972); Reprinted in *Vox Africana* nos. 7,8 & 9. (1972).

117. M. Meredith, *The State of Africa: A History of Fifty Years of Independence* (London: Free Press, 2005) 59.

118. Curtin, *The Image of Africa*, 425.

119. D.N. Levine, "Simmel at a Distance: On the History and Systematics of the Sociology of the Stranger," in *Strangers in African Societies* ed. W.A. Shack and E.P. Skinner (Berkeley: University of California Press, 1979) 21-36.

120. Mills, *The Racial Contract*, 119.

121. H. Ochwada, "Historians, Nationalism and Pan-Africanism: Myths and Realities" in *African Intellectuals: Rethinking Politics, Language, Gender and Development*. ed. T. Mkandawire. (New York: Zed Books, 2005) 200.

122. J.S. Mbiti, *African Religions and Philosophy* (Oxford: Heinemann Educational Publishers, 1989) 261.

123. Ibid., 262.

124. S.B. Biko, "Black Consciousness and the Quest for a True Humanity" in *The African Philosophy Reader*. ed. P.H. Coetzee and A.P.J. Roux (London: Routledge) 81.

125. Ibid.

126. Ochwada, "Historians, Nationalism and Pan-Africanism" 195.

127. Sherlock, *Jamaica's Proud Heritage*, 9.

128. Undated publication of the KODIC (Kenneth Onwuka Dike Centre) based in Awka, Nigeria..

129. Alagoa, *The Practice of History in Africa*, 45.

130. A.E. Afigbo, "The Poverty of African Historiography" (Lagos: Afrografika Publishers 1977).

131. Ibid., 196.

132. Undated publication of the KODIC.

133. Cited in Ochwada, "Historians, Nationalism and Pan-Africanism." 194.

134. Jomo Kenyatta, *Facing Mount Kenya* (London: Heinemann 1979).

135. C. Williams, *The Destruction of Black Civilization: Great Issues of a Race from 4500 BC to 2000 AD* (Chicago, Illinois: Third World Press, 1987) 18.

136. Alagoa, *The Practice of History in Africa*, 140.

137. Mkandawire, "Introduction," 6.

138. Society of African Culture, "The death of Cheik Anta Diop" *Prensence Africaine*, no. 136, (4th Quarter, 1985) 8-9; also cited in Alagoa, *The Practice of History*, 140.

139. Akbar, *Breaking the Chains of Psychological Slavery*, 35.

140. Ochwada, "Historians, Nationalism and Pan-Africanism," 198.

141. Mkandawire, "African Intellectuals and Nationalism," 27.

142. K. Thomas, "'Ain't Nothin Like the Real Thing': Black Masculinity, Gay Sexuality, and the Jargon of Authenticity," in *The House that Race Built*. ed. W. Lubiano (New York: Vintage Books, 1998) 124.

143. K. Anthony Appiah, *In My Father's House: Africa in the Philosophy of Culture* (Oxford: Oxford Univ. Press, 1992) 178.

144. A. Conway, *The History of the Negro in the United States* (London: The Historical Association of London, no 67, 1968); also see: H. Hampton and S. Fayer, *Voices of Freedom: An Oral History of the Civil Rights Movement from the 1950s through the 1980s* (New York: Banton Books, 1990).

145. T. Ngugi, *Decolonizing the Mind: The Politics of Language in African Literature* (Oxford: James Currey Reprint, 2005) 88.

REVIEW
AND/OR
RESPONSE-ESSAYS
TO THE
INAUGURAL
ADDRES

RACE, SLAVERY
AND IMPERIALISM

KNOWLEDGE
PRODUCTION
AND PERSONHOOD

- DMITRI VAN DAN BERSSELAAR -

Prominently displayed in Liverpool's International Slavery Museum is a large photograph which seems to speak to many of the issues raised in Professor Wariboko's thought-provoking essay. It is an enlargement of a Christmas staff photograph of a British trading company operating in Nigeria.[1] It shows three rows of bare-chested African workers posing for the camera. Each man's chest is painted (adorned!) with a letter to spell out "1923 Badagry Merry Xmas." Four Europeans, dressed in white, sit on a makeshift bench upfront together with three young Africans, possibly domestic servants. No one in the image looks merry. The photograph was taken at the height of British colonial rule in Nigeria when, following World War I, local colonial administration was (re)established and the export-produce-based economy was also booming ahead of the crisis of the 1930s. These were years when the colonial government could afford to invest part of its growing revenue from customs duties and—increasingly—direct taxation in the "civilising mission," attempting to improve local government, building infrastructure, and wrestling control over African education away from the missionaries. The Europeans in the photograph were, of course, not part of the colonial administration. However, through their activities and attitudes they were very much part of the colonial project.[2]

The contrast between the clothed Europeans in the foreground and the mostly bare-chested Africans, who fill out the rest of the photograph, appears to reflect the link in imperialist ideology between "race," colonialism and the notion of the "civilising mission." This possibility is however immediately undermined by the staggering inappropriateness of this image, produced to be sent out to business contacts, family and friends in Europe. This is, perhaps, even more so the case when we realise that someone might have thought of this as a harmless and "nice" idea in keeping with the spirit of Christmas. The nonchalant way in which in this photograph African bodies were used and subjected to the gaze of the Europeans, draws attention to other ways in which Europeans have been exploiting African bodies—from the inception of the transatlantic trade in enslaved Africans, to the produce-based economy during colonialism. It is thus not surprising that this colonial image—produced 116 years after the abolition of the transatlantic slave trade, and 85 years after the ending of slavery in the Americas—is so prominently displayed in the International Slavery Museum. Its display also reminds us of the complexity of the history of race and racism: concepts shaped as much by the histories of slavery and the slave trade, as by imperialism and colonial rule.[3] The politics of knowledge production and the debates associated with New World slavery and post-slavery influenced the construction of black personhood in Africa through their impact on imperialist ideology, and also through their impact on black anti-slavery and post-slavery thinkers. A further, and more problematic, connection exists through the link between abolitionist thought and imperialist ideology.

Through exploring the connections that can be seen in the photograph, and by reflecting on their meanings, this contribution will expand Professor Wariboko's thesis in two directions: first, the need to include the racist ideology that emerged in the context of the transatlantic slave trade among the factors that influenced articulations of black personhood in Africa and elsewhere; second, the need to consider how historically specific local traditions of colonial knowledge production—that could differ from those from the imperial centre in significant details—fed into local identities in colonial and postcolonial Africa. The contribution will explore in turn: the link between abolitionist thought and imperialist ideology; the impact of the Atlantic slavery complex on the thinking of leading West African nationalists; the transfer of knowledge and ideology within the British empire, including the relationship between imperial propaganda in the metropolis and the development of local traditions of colonial knowledge; the importance of local and individual circumstances; and the connections between the "civilising mission," personhood, and consumption.

At the beginning of the nineteenth century, prominent members of the movement to abolish the transatlantic slave trade argued that African societies had been brutalised through their involvement in the slave trade. In their view, centuries of slave raiding and kidnapping had resulted in widespread distrust, had destroyed morality, and had made it impossible for government to emerge and for civilisation to occur. These abolitionists argued that black people needed civilising. However, this was not because they were biologically inferior, but because of their experienced history. Thus, out of a humanitarian impulse, an ideology of interventionism emerged, which would eventually end up supporting imperialism. Anti-slavery also contributed to the gendered discourse of imperialism through its focus on the perceived slave status of women in African societies, exploited and oppressed by what was described as "brutal males," which contributed to the definition of these societies as "savage."[4] Arguments for intervention became even stronger after the abolition of the British slave trade in 1807, because slave exports continued from outside British controlled ports, while African internal slave systems persisted and even expanded. In response to this, anti-slavery campaigners proceeded to gather and publicise evidence on African slavery and slave trading.[5] In doing so they aided the ending of slavery, but also contributed to the building up of stereotypes of Africans as "savage" and in need of being saved and civilised by Europeans. Intervention was part of a number of actual and proposed strategies to stop the illegal slave trade. Well known amongst these were the British and the French naval squadrons stationed off the coast of West Africa, which attempted to intercept slave trading vessels.[6] Also important was the support for what was now called "legitimate trade," conducted through European trading houses, as it was expected that the development of the trade in agricultural produce would reduce the incentive for

Africans to continue slave trading.[7] Thus British trading in West Africa came to be regarded as ethical again, helping to lift Africans out of the misery of slavery and bringing civilisation instead. The commodities imported into Africa therefore had to be "civilising goods" such as cloth and clothing, cutlery, and tools.[8] The nineteenth century also saw a number of anti-slavery expeditions which had intended, among other things, to sign anti-slavery treaties with African leaders and to promote trade and Christianity. In addition, there were the activities of a number of missionary organisations which aimed to end slavery through moral uplift.[9] It is worth noting that, although there was a slow and gradual process of colonial expansion from the European coastal trading enclaves, nearly all of West Africa was independent during the nineteenth century. From around 1880, due to a number of factors, European occupation and colonization of Africa accelerated in leaps and bounds. During the second half of that century, the continuation of slave trading was the justification for many instances of colonial conquest by European powers, including the British annexation of Lagos in 1861.[10]

It was not just the imperialist ideology of race that was at least partly informed by the Atlantic slavery complex, so were the ideologies of leading West African nationalists who resisted imperialism. West African thinkers such as J. E. Casely Hayford explicitly referred to the American (post-)slavery experience in their writings on race and imperialism.[11] A number of these thinkers were born in the Americas and already had considerable exposure to African American discourse on race prior to their arrival in West Africa. This category includes one of the most influential nineteenth-century African nationalists, Edward Wilmot Blyden. Blyden was born on the Caribbean island of St Thomas (then under Danish rule), spent a couple of years in Venezuela with his parents, and moved to the United States when he was 18 years old. He stayed in the United States for three years, where he met a number of religious leaders involved in the African Colonization Society. Encouraged by them he went to Liberia in 1853, to work as a lay preacher and teacher. During the years he lived and worked in Liberia and Sierra Leone, Blyden published a number of highly influential books and pamphlets on race and pan-Africanism. He advocated the return to Africa of educated "pure Negroes" from America who would lead the continent to freedom. Disappointed by their failure to do so, Blyden came instead to regard European colonial rule as a necessary phase in African development, and he consequently supported British expansion in West Africa.[12] It is worth noting that this nationalist, with all his black credentials, saw Africa as being in need of civilization through outside intervention. This viewpoint was not uncommon at the time. In 1868 James Africanus Horton made the same recommendation in his influential book, *West African Countries and Peoples*.[13] Before this, it was common for North American back-to-Africa movements—which had influenced Blyden in the early 1850s, and which were themselves influenced by abolitionist thought—to consider Africa as "a fallen civilisation to be redeemed by African American Christians."[14] These views had changed by the first half of the twentieth century, but the call for African Americans to come to Africa continued. An influential Jamaican-born Nigerian nationalist during this period was Amos Shackleford, who arrived in Lagos in 1913 when he was 26 years old. In Nigeria he was successful as a businessman and as a nationalist thinker and politician. He co-founded Nigeria's first major political party and was an active participant in the movement founded by Marcus Garvey, serving as the president of the Lagos branch of the Universal Negro Improvement Association and the African Communities League.[15] In addition to those who came over from the Americas, there were also West Africans who went to the United States and developed their outlook on race and racism there. This group included J. Abayomi Cole, who was born in Nigeria in the 1840s and travelled to the United States in the 1880s, where he experienced racism which led him to the conclusion that the Western claim of liberty was false. Like Blyden, he wanted African Americans to come to Africa to educate Africans.[16] Another example is Orishatukeh Faduma, who spent most of his childhood in Sierra Leone, went to school and university in Britain for a couple of years in the 1880s, and travelled to America for further studies in the 1890s. He married an African American and worked in the United States as a teacher and missionary for seventeen years. His ideas on race and pan-Africanism were shaped by his American experience, and he was active in the back-to-Africa movement, arguing that: "It is certainly better for American Negroes to die of African fever in the effort to contribute to Africa's development than to be riddled by the bullets of white mobs that control the local governments of the United States."[17]

The imperialist theory of race, with its protocols of imperial knowledge production, which developed during the nineteenth century, as described by Professor Wariboko, thus emerged against a complex background. This included, in no particular order, the British experience of colonial rule in India; the history of race and (post-)slavery in the Americas; the anti-slavery movements in Europe (and the United States); and, finally, the frequent transatlantic contacts of black intellectuals. An examination of these complex patterns of relations allows us to expand on two important points that Professor Wariboko made in his essay: first, the importance of the transfer of knowledge and ideology within the empire, not just from Britain to Africa, but also from India to Africa and from the Caribbean to Africa; second, the distinction between imperial propaganda in the metropolis and the development of local traditions of imperial knowledge and propaganda. Imperial knowledge in general demonised blackness and infantilised indigenous peoples to provide a justification for conquest and subsequently for continued colonial rule.[18] Those who produced local level colonial knowledge nevertheless had to find ways to look beyond what Mudimbe has called "the syndrome of savagery" in order to be able to come up with information that would be useful for colonial policy formulation on the local level.[19] In Africa, the most pervasive and powerful method of producing local colonial knowledge was ethnography, which aimed to describe and classify pre-colonial societies. The prominence of this type of knowledge reflected the intention to graft colonial administration onto existing traditional authorities. The colonial administration needed to know the extent and boundaries of the traditional political units, the political organisation of these units, the influence of traditional religion, and the legitimate leaders of the traditional political units. Following the nineteenth-century logic of a hierarchy of races, in India, the administration assumed that the requisite facts could be discovered through history.[20] In Africa, the same function was provided by local ethnographies. The different needs of imperialist propaganda in the metropolis and local colonial governments, however, gave rise to contradictions within the imperialist discourse. For example, while local ethnographies, ethnographic questionnaires, and correspondence between colonial administrators, were attempting to identify African leaders that could be incorporated into the colonial system as trusted intermediaries, some metropolitan newspapers, such as the *London Illustrated News*, and colonial exhibitions, were representing African leaders as uncivilised, corrupt savages.[21] Over time, specific local circumstances (such as the differences in the make-up of colonial administrations in Northern Nigeria and Southern Nigeria),[22] resulted in local traditions of colonial knowledge production that could in crucial aspects differ from that devised in the metropolis. Similar processes were at work in the knowledge production that took place in the context of missionary enterprise. Professor Wariboko has already drawn our attention to the use of missionary journals and correspondence as a source of content for the printed materials that missionary organisations such as the Church

Missionary Society (CMS) produced to inform their supporters in the United Kingdom on whom they relied for the funding of their civilising projects in Africa. The articles in publications such as *The Church Missionary Record* and *The Church Missionary Intelligencer* alleged that African societies were "savage"—rife with human sacrifice, war, violence and crime, polygamy and nakedness. However, local missionary knowledge of African societies had to look for those aspects of African religions onto which Christianity could be grafted, as well as aspects that were not contrary to Christian belief and were therefore acceptable for African Christian converts.[23] While written for different publics, the contents of the metropolitan imperialist propaganda did in fact reach at least some members of the African public. This occurred partly through the West African nationalist writers who, in one way or another, had personally encountered the metropolitan perspective while in Britain, France, or Germany. They also read the metropolitan newspapers that were sent out to West Africa, and critically discussed their contents in the local West African press. Similarly, copies of the evangelical publications were sent out to the African mission stations where they appeared to have received a mixed reception. Igbo-speaking school pupils, according to one of the CMS missionaries, "see all the CMS papers, and do not like what is in the *Children's World*. They say it is making fun of their country."[24] However, locally produced colonial knowledge was not necessarily liked better. When in 1936 C. K. Meek, the government anthropologist for Southern Nigeria, produced a "Report on the Social and Political Organisations in Owerri Division" the contents of the report quickly became known in the local communities even though it had not been published or circulated. Before long, the chief commissioner had received a letter complaining that "throughout Mr Meek's Report all that is said about your petitioners—the Osu family group—is, to our mind, motivated by spite and prejudice, and with the avowed aim of exposing your petitioners to public contempt, ridicule and shame." The letter continued by asserting that "by collecting information about your petitioners from prejudicial sources, and by failing to consult any member of our own family group in order to confirm or refute the points adduced, your petitioners maintain that the molestation and injustice to which they have been subjected are innumerable and uncalled for."[25]

The "Badagry Merry Christmas" photograph can thus be used to explore "race" and its links with slavery and the imperialist ideology over time and throughout the Empire. However, the image also invites us to consider the importance of place and local circumstances—the particular. Badagry, which by the 1920s had become one of the lesser ports in the produce trade, has an auspicious history. It had been an important slave trading port from the 1730s until the late eighteenth century, and slaves continued to be exported from Badagry well into the nineteenth century, albeit in smaller numbers; the last recorded slaving vessel left the port in 1845.[26] However, when liberated Yoruba slaves from Sierra Leone began to return to their homeland, Badagry was the place where they first settled (after the first group had been attacked and robbed attempting to land at Lagos).[27] Badagry is also regarded as the place where Christianity was first preached in Nigeria, as the Wesleyan Missionary Society opened a station at Badagry in 1842, and the CMS followed suit in 1845. Most of the early missionaries were black people recruited in Sierra Leone or the Caribbean. As Professor Wariboko notes in his essay, they "were phenotypically black; but they did not identify themselves as culturally black." This contrasts markedly with the attitude of other West Indians who came to West Africa during this period, such as Shackleford and Blyden, and Sierra Leoneans such as Cole and Faduma, all of whom had a strong sense of their black personhood and can be regarded as African nationalists and even as pan-Africanists. While all of these West Indians and Sierra Leoneans were the beneficiaries of the missionary and colonial school systems which, as Professor Wariboko argues had, "constituted the most potent instruments for introducing and entrenching white normativity in African societies," the main differentiating feature might have been exposure in the United States to (post)slavery racism and to African American cultural nationalism.

How the imperialist discourse on blackness and the civilising mission is consumed, is thus dependent on local and individual circumstances. This can also be illustrated with the example of the "Hamitic Hypothesis." The idea that West African peoples were descendants from the Jews of the "Old Testament" was fairly widespread in missionary and in colonial circles during the nineteenth century and the first half of the twentieth century. This idea had its roots in an older, eighteenth-century version of the "Hamitic Hypothesis." According to that version, the black peoples of Africa descended from Noah's son Ham, whose offspring had been divinely cursed to a life of servitude. This early "Hamitic Hypothesis" was refined a number of times, primarily to "whiten" the Egyptians; and by the 1920s, the "Hamitic Hypothesis" had come to denote the colonial idea that, throughout the history of Africa, it had been lighter-skinned peoples who had inspired civilisation into black peoples. This notion was widely used in popular and scholarly literature as a justification for European colonial rule until World War II.[28] Meanwhile, for many specific West African ethnic groups, an earlier version of the "Hamitic Hypothesis," which merely claimed their "Jewish origins," had become adopted in missionary ethnographies, and also in a number of local histories.[29] Thus the notion of Hebrew origins had become an important feature of local traditions of colonial knowledge production. The idea that the particular people they were trying to convert had "originally" been Jewish was particularly appealing to missionaries. The concept that monotheism lay at the basis of the religious system of the particular ethnic group, but had gradually been lost or diminished—for instance, as a result of distortions brought about by a reliance on oral transmission of customs through the ages[30]—gave missionaries both a justification and a starting-point for conversion.[31]

The English CMS missionary G. T. Basden, who spent his entire career as a missionary in the northern Igbo area, was strongly convinced that the Igbo had descended from the Jews. During a career spanning more than thirty years, Basden published two books and numerous articles, in each of these he discussed or at least mentioned the similarities between Igbo customs and the customs of the Jews of the "Old Testament." Basden's work, especially his first book, *Among the Ibos of Nigeria*,[32] is still well known in Eastern Nigeria and widely consulted by Igbo scholars. Thus while Hebrew origins in general became part of the imperialist discourse, the way the concept has been locally consumed by the Igbo-speaking peoples and by a broad coalition of Igbo intellectuals, has turned it into a local knowledge tradition, with many Igbo-speaking individuals claiming Jewish origins as part of their black personhood.

A final aspect of the "civilising mission" and of black personhood that is raised by the "Merry Christmas" photograph is that of consumption. The contrast between the painted, naked black torsos, and the clothed Europeans, reminds us of the colonial—and missionary—interpretation of civilisation as a transition from nakedness to clothing. By the 1920s the consumption of manufactured goods had become strongly linked to colonial ideas of a civilising mission.[33] Colonial governments argued that the desire for more and better goods was a central characteristic of a civilised society, to justify their promotion of monetisation and the consumption by Africans of "appropriate goods" such as clothing, soap, and bicycles.[34] As with other aspects of the civilising mission, the spread of monetisation and consumption was subject to this inherent contradiction in colonial ideology: the fundamental tension between the need to view the colonial subject as fundamentally different and yet somewhat similar. The "Otherness" of the colonised—their perceived "primitive," "uncivilised" and "lawless" state—served as one of the justifications for colonisation. However, if the civilising mission proved successful, this would undermine the rationale for continued colonial occupation.[35] Therefore, whenever Africans accepted and exhibited the colonisers' patterns of consumption, they were in fact challenging colonialism. In response, as with education and employment, colonialism attempted to regulate and limit African consumptive ambitions. This was plainly visible in the area of clothing. Missionaries and colonisers had used "nakedness" as an image representing the "primitive" state of Africans before colonisation, and encouraged the covering of African bodies with imported clothes as evidence of civilisation.[36] Yet those Africans who showed too much knowledge and sophistication in their wearing of European-style clothing were criticised for being insufficiently "native."[37] G. T. Basden had written already in 1915 that Africans wearing a suit, tie, and hat, paid no attention to the demands of the African climate and were merely being ignorant imitators of Europeans. The colonial contradiction is evident in his warning that with these well-dressed Africans, "it is not always easy to remember that we are dealing with a child race, and that all the vagaries and waywardness of children must be expected."[38] African nationalists did not necessarily disagree. In *Ethiopia Unbound*, Casely Hayford had emphasised that Africans should dress according to African cultural norms, rather than European ones. Writing in 1911, Casely Hayford already anticipated the point that Basden would make four years later, when he warned that, "[w]ithout servile imitation of our teachers in their get-up and manner of life, it stands to reason that the average white man would regard the average black man far more seriously than he does at present."[39]

In addition to a concern with encouraging Africans to make appropriate consumptive choices, colonial economies also steered African consumption through the marketing of cheap versions of commodities, "for natives only." The importation of relatively inexpensive commodities for sale to Africans dates back to the pre-colonial period, and initially reflected a demand for goods that were affordable to African agricultural producers with limited cash. During the colonial period, such cheap commodities acquired additional meanings, reflecting racial difference and domination. Throughout colonial Africa, the availability of specific commodities was one of the ways through which racial superiority was constructed. Timothy Burke has discussed the example of inexpensive "red" soaps that were sold to African consumers throughout the continent. After explaining that this type of soap has a distinctive, unforgettable smell because of the added disinfectant carbolic, Burke observes: "Given the established weight of the settler vision of 'dirty' Africans, it is unsurprising that soaps with extra disinfectant, soaps that give users a distinctive odour connoting cleanliness, were thought by white manufacturers to be particularly appropriate for use by Africans."[40] For African consumers, meanwhile, the circumstance of a commodity being foreign, or being used by white people, made that commodity more attractive. However, the colonial context required that, generally, Europeans expressed their superiority through the consumption of superior brands and types of goods, and therefore these superior commodities could not be marketed explicitly to African consumers. This was less critical in West Africa than in areas with European settlers, such as South and East Africa, where the racially labelled consumption of daily commodities helped to define a class of poor whites as being somehow superior to the African population.

The decolonisation years of the 1950s and 1960s posed a challenge to the colonial ideology of consumption, even though the connection that this ideology had established between consumption and "civilisation" continued for decades after independence. Thus the link continued between the consumption of appropriate (often foreign) commodities and "being civilised," but Africans were no longer limited to "inferior" goods. Of course, wealthy Africans had frequently ignored such constraints during the colonial period, which had resulted in them being treated with suspicion by the colonial authorities. The nationalist press noted that such limitations no longer applied to "Africans of modern times." A letter published in the *West African Pilot* asserted in 1954 that: "It is from this clothes-wearing class, the civilized class, that health, progress, education and general improvement can be found."[41]

It is thus clear that the articulation of black personhood did not only take place in the context of the imperialist ideology and knowledge production, but also through the contested consumption by Africans of the commodities of empire. Through their consumptive practices Africans throughout the colonial period challenged a colonial ideology of consumption thought applicable to subject peoples. However, the link between civilisation and particular forms of consumption continued long after the colonial period, when independent African elites would attempt to appropriate the consumptive practices of the former colonial powers.

The connections between "race," the "civilising mission," blackness and African personhood are complex and multi-faceted. They include the racist myths and theories of the imperialists, and also the appropriations and re-interpretations of such notions by local African intellectuals. They thus include general theories of race and imperialism, and specific local articulations. They also include connections between the imperialist ideology of nineteenth and twentieth century colonialism in Africa, and the racist ideologies that emerged out of plantation slavery in the Atlantic. We thus need to acknowledge the Atlantic as a space through which travelled many of the people and ideas that helped to develop African personhood, often in competition with colonial knowledge production about Africans.

Notes

1. The caption in the museum (derived from the information provided in the Images of Empire photograph database of The British Empire and Commonwealth Museum) identifies the company as "The African Oil Nuts Company and Miller Brothers." The African Oil Nuts Company had started trading in Nigeria during World War I, but not much is known about this business. Miller Brothers (of Liverpool) Limited had been established in 1907 and in 1919 had merged with other companies to form The African and Eastern Trade Corporation Ltd, but continued to trade under the Miller Brothers name. In the following years a number of other companies trading in West Africa were acquired, but it is not clear whether this may have included the African Oil Nuts Company (certainly not direct, but it may have been acquired at an earlier stage by a company subsequently acquired by the African and Eastern Trade Corporation). See: F. Pedler, *The Lion and the Unicorn in Africa: A History of the Origins of the United Africa Company 1787-1931* (London: Heinemann, 1974).

2. T. Falola and M.M. Heaton, *A History of Nigeria* (Cambridge: Cambridge University Press, 2008) 118-34.

3. B. Fields, "Slavery, race and ideology in the United States of America," *New Left Review* 181 (1990) 95-118; F. Cooper & R. Brubaker, "Identity" in *Colonialism in Question: Theory, Knowledge, History*. ed. F. Cooper (Berkeley, L A: University of California Press, 2005) 59-90.

4. C. Midgley, "'Anti-slavery and the roots of "imperial feminism"'" in *Gender and Imperialism*. ed. C. Midgley (Manchester: Manchester University Press, 1998) 161-79.

5. W. Ackerson, *The African Institution (1807-1827) and the Antislavery Movement in Great Britain* (Lewiston: Edwin Mellen Press, 2005).

6. T. R. Getz, *Slavery and Reform in West Africa: Towards Emancipation in Nineteenth-Century Senegal and the Gold Coast* (Athens: Ohio University Press, 2004) 30-4.

7.   R. Law, "Introduction" in *From Slave Trade to 'Legitimate' Commerce. The Commercial Transition in Nineteenth-Century West Africa.* ed. R. Law (Cambridge: Cambridge University Press, 1995) 1-31.

8.   For this reason, anti-slavery campaigners and missionaries strongly objected to the importation of rum and gin. See: D.V.D. Bersselaar, *The King of Drinks: Schnapps Gin from Modernity to Tradition* (Leiden: Brill, 2007) 10.

9.   H. Temperley, *White Dreams, Black Africa: The Antislavery Expedition to the Niger 1841-1842* (New Haven: Yale University Press, 1991) 15-25 & 58.

10. K. Mann, *Slavery and the Birth of an African City: Lagos, 1760-1900* (Bloomington: Indiana University Press, 2007) 101.

11. J. E. Casely-Hayford, *Ethiopia Unbound* (London: C. M. Phillips, 1911) 174-5.

12. H.C.G.. Matthew, "Blyden, Edward Wilmot (1832–1912)," *Oxford Dictionary of National Biography* (Oxford:Oxford University Press, 2004) [http://www.oxforddnb.com/view/article/69732, accessed 30 May 2009].

13. J.A.B. Horton, *West African Countries and Peoples, British and Native: with the Requirements Necessary for Establishing that Self Government Recommended by the Committee of the House of Commons, 1865; and a Vindication of the African Race* (London: W. J. Johnson, 1868).

14. Cooper & Brubaker, "Identity," 84.

15. T. Falola, *Nationalism and African Intellectuals* (Rochester: University of Rochester Press, 2001) 60.

16. Ibid., 62 & 82.

17. Orishatukeh Faduma, quoted in Falola, *Nationalism and African Intellectuals*, 84.

18. N. Thomas, *Colonialism's Culture: Anthropology, Travel and Government* (Cambridge: Polity Press, 1994) 134.

19. V. Y. Mudimbe, *The Invention of Africa. Gnosis, Philosophy and the Order of Knowledge* (Bloomington: Indiana University Press, 1988) 49.

20. B. Cohn, *Colonialism and its Forms of Knowledge: The British in India* (Princeton: Princeton University Press, 1996) 5.

21. A. Coombes, *Reinventing Africa: Museums, Material Culture and Popular Imagination* (New Haven: Yale University Press, 1994) 129-60; R. L. Tignor, "Political corruption in Nigeria before independence," *Journal of Modern African Studies*, 31.2 (1993) 175-202.

22. I.F. Nicolson, *The Administration of Nigeria 1900-1960: Men, Methods and Myths* (Oxford: Clarendon Press, 1969).

23. B. Meyer, *Translating the Devil: Religion and Modernity among the Ewe in Ghana* (Edinburgh: Edinburgh University Press, 1999) 61.

24. F. K. Ekechi, *Missionary Enterprise and Rivalry in Igboland* (London: Frank Cass, 1972) 80.

25. Nigeria National Archive Ibadan CSO 26/27948, "Petition from Members of the family group of Umuoronjo Compound of Owerri Town to the Chief Commissioner, Southern Provinces, Enugu, Owerri" 22 May 1936 .

26. Mann, *Slavery and the Birth of an African City*, 34; R. Law, *Ouidah: The Social History of a West African Slaving 'Port' 1727-1892* (Oxford: James Currey, 2004) 125-7; *Voyages. The Transatlantic Slave Trade Database* [http://www.slavevoyages.org/tast/database/search.faces, accessed 31 May 2009].

27. Mann, *Slavery and the Birth of an African City*, 92.

28. The history of the "Hamitic Hypothesis" is discussed in detail in Zachernuk, "Of Origins and Colonial Order"; on the use of the idea in colonial historiography see: A.E. Afigbo, "Colonial historiography" in *African Historiography: Essays in Honour of Jacob Ade Ajayi*. ed. T. Falola (Harlow and Ikeja: Longman, 1993), 39-51.

29. R. Law, "Constructing 'a real national history': a comparison of Edward Blyden and Samuel Johnson" in *Self-Assertion and*

Brokerage. Early Cultural Nationalism in West Africa. eds. K. Barber & P.F. de Moraes Farias. (Birmingham: Centre for West African Studies, 1990) 78-100; R. Law, "The 'Hamitic hypothesis' in indigenous West African historical thought," *History in Africa* 36 (2009), 293-314.

30. G. T. Basden, *Niger Ibos: A Description of the Primitive Life, Customs and Animistic Beliefs etc., of the Ibo People of Nigeria by One Who, for Thirty-Five years, Enjoyed the Privilege of their Intimate Confidence and Friendship* (London: Seeley, Service and Co., 1938; reprinted: London: Frank Cass, 1966) 413.

31. Meyer, *Translating the Devil*, 60-2.

32. G. T. Basden, *Among the Ibos of Nigeria: An Account of the Curious and Interesting Habits, Customs and Beliefs of a Little-Known African People by One who has for Many Years Lived Amongst them on Close and Intimate Terms* (London: Seeley, Service and Co., 1921).

33. T. Richards, *The Commodity Culture of Victorian England: Advertising and Spectacle, 1851-1914* (Stanford: Stanford University Press, 1990) 123.

34. T. Burke, *Lifebuoy Men, Lux Women: Commodification, Consumption, and Cleanliness in Modern Zimbabwe* (London: Leicester University Pres, 1996) 2, 84-5.

35. Mudimbe, *The Invention of Africa*; H. Bhabha, *The Location of Culture* (London: Routledge, 1994); Thomas, *Colonialism's Culture*; A. Loomba, *Colonialism/Postcolonialism* (London: Routledge, 1998). In using the term "colonial contradiction" I follow Nugent's clear formulation of this phenomenon. See: Paul Nugent, *Africa Since Independence* (Basingstoke: Pallgrave Macmillan, 2004).

36. Mudimbe, *The Invention of Africa*.

37. J. Rich, "Civilized attire: refashioning tastes and social status in the Gabon Estuary, c. 1870-1914" *Cultural and Social History* 2 (2005) 202.

38. G.T. Basden, "Denationalizing a primitive people," *Church Missionary Review* (October 1915) 726.

39. Casely Hayford, *Ethiopia Unbound*, 175.

40. Burke, *Lifebuoy Men, Lux Women*, 151.

41. Letter to the editor by R. I. Nnoka, *West African Pilot*, 22 July 1954.

CHRISTIAN MISSIONARIES, RACISM, AND THE EMERGENCE OF AN AFRICAN HISTORIOGRAPHY OF 'SELF-DAMNATION'

- RAPHAEL C. NJOKU -

———•———

This is a response to an inaugural address by Professor Waibinte Elekima Wariboko on the occasion of his promotion to full professorship at the University of the West Indies, Mona Campus-Jamaica. The seminal address by one of Africa's most engaging historians of our time dwelled on the intersection between European Christian missionary activities—precisely their perceptions of Africa—and how this led to Western invention of a derogatory African identity and personhood over the period of colonial rule. Although previous studies have discussed this issue at length, Wariboko's approach is important because it straddles the divide between events that took place on the continent and those witnessed outside. Additionally, Wariboko elucidates how the alien demonization of Africa's culture and society gave birth to a nationalist form of historical narrative geared towards self-assertion. That nationalist approach, in my interpretation, has also been misused by some scholars in perpetuating similar abuses wrought by the European agents of race and the civilizing mission.

Born in Nigeria and trained at institutions in Nigeria and the United Kingdom, Wariboko drank from the rich scholarly fountains of prominent Africanist historians like Robin Horton, Ebiegberi Joseph Alagoa, and Tom MacCaskie, to mention but a few. He started his teaching appointment at the University of Port Harcourt in Nigeria from where he moved, in 1993, to the Mona Campus of the University of the West Indies in Jamaica on a Technical Assistance Program (TAC). Wariboko has since impressed his former teachers, professional colleagues, students and other interested readers, with his grounded knowledge and mastery of African and African diaspora historiography. This attests to his meteoric rise from the position of a visiting lecturer to a tenured professor. Wariboko's erudite and award-winning monographs and scholarly articles have covered diverse topics ranging from slavery, leadership, ethnicity, colonialism, missionary evangelism, and African diaspora history. Having read most of these books and long essays; having had the pleasure of observing his presentations at academic meetings; and having had the honor to work with him on a project on *Missions, States, and European Expansion in Africa*, it is my humble opinion that only a handful of scholars can match his demonstrated knowledge in the field of Christian missionary history.[1] Wariboko uses archival and library resources, including oral testimonies, to produce original works; and his prudent methodological and epistemological approaches make him a historian's-historian.

While Wariboko's interests are spread across diverse fields of African studies and African diaspora studies, the subject closest to his heart remains the intersection between

the European civilizing mission and the ideological construction of race as it affects blackness and the African
identity. Race, religion, and the African identity are intertwined in the eternal struggle for emancipation. As Wariboko illuminated in his *Ruined by "Race,"* which focused on
Afro-Caribbean missionaries in Southern Nigeria, race and
racism inspired the European missionary efforts in Africa
and this mindset also ruined the primary goal of Christian
evangelism—namely, the conversion of souls.[2] In Africa and
elsewhere, the "civilizing mission" had played a diabolical role
in casting "blackness" and Africanness as inferior, while promoting "whiteness" as superior.

But it is crucial to understand that the brand of Christianity introduced to the Africans was corrupted principally by
one thing: European race pride and egoism that had in part
emanating from the successes of the Industrial Revolution
(c. 1775-1885). Carefully considered, the racialist invention of Africa, including the efforts to evangelize Africans,
were all greatly informed by the comparative imbalance in
technological development between industrialized Europe
and predominantly agrarian Africa. In the century that suc-
ceeded the Industrial Revolution, Europeans had sat back to
reflect on their path-breaking inventions in communication,
transportation, modern medicine, military hardware, industrial merchandize, and lots more. The natural tendency was
for them to claim superiority over other races.

Given the ideological factors that were at work in the
cultural politics of knowledge production, including their
implications for the uses and/or abuses of anthropological,
ethnographic, historical and socio-linguistic evidence, the
evolving imperial historiography effectively glorified "whiteness" as opposed to "blackness." Such ethnic chauvinism
overlooked several pertinent facts. One, the capital accumulation that made it possible for Europe to jump ahead,
technologically, came from the enormous profitability of the
slave trade in earlier centuries. Two, it was the sophistication

of West African farming techniques brought to the Americas by African slaves, that gave the European financiers the capital needed to industrialize their countries while saving the Americas from bankruptcy. Three, the European "I-am-better-than-you" attitude towards the African implied that the latter's life could be dispensed with, if it could not be salvaged from its supposed sub-human condition. Not surprisingly, this way of thinking brought about the colonial intrusion that was marked by deadly violence throughout the African continent.

Today, no honest observer could challenge a sobering truth. The economic undertones of colonialism were hidden under the garb of philanthropy and criminal notions of spiritual salvation. Concerned more with a new form of capitalist accumulation, the Europeans demonized the African personhood in order to justify and to hide the blatant economic motive of colonialism. The printing presses cranked out tones of pseudoscientific literatures on Africa to influence and shape the world's perception of Africa and Africans as savage and benighted. Unfortunately, Africans did not have the benefit of printing technology to make their voices heard, their histories put straight and aright, until several decades of colonial rule when the first generation of the educated elite began to articulate their local histories in the context of decolonization.

African Nationalist History and the Abuse of Evidence

The era of decolonization provided an opportunity for the emergent African educated elite to challenge the colonial historiography and the forms of racism it enthroned. The institutionalization of an African nationalist historiography was in the spirit of the era of decolonization. The crux of the "New Historiography," or what Wariboko has identified here as the "Historiography of Self-Assertion," was to assert the true African identity and personhood. In the process, Wariboko aptly observes the tendency towards an abuse of evidence inherent in the historiography of self-assertion.

There is a widespread characterization of the educated African elite, particularly the immediate inheritors of the postcolonial state, as individuals who were alienated from their people in the mainstream historical literature under review. I wish to interrogate and elaborate a little on this characterization from the standpoint of the pro-alienation discourse. Within the pro-alienation discourse, the term alienation has been conceptually and contextually abused in relation to the African colonial elite and their postcolonial leadership of the continent. "The Historiography of Self-assertion," in this sense, has failed not only to see alienation as a common social problem in all human societies. It has tended also to assert only the negative interpretations without much reference to the positive and value neutral meanings of alienation. In their misjudgments, scholars of the pro-alienation school have seen "alienation" simplistically as a problem of an elite/mass gap; this difference, the school has also argued, explains the leadership failures in the continent associated with these persons.

This kind of reductionism is implicit in Coleman's *Nigeria: Background to Nationalism*.[3] In sympathy with the continued exclusion of a significant number of well-educated Africans from the top colonial administrative positions, Coleman perceived the emergent Nigerian elite as those being trapped in a "dualism [which] created frustration and bitterness."[4] Pushing the "alienation" thesis, Coleman describes the political colonial elite as non-cultural nativists (i.e. individuals extricated from their cultures) and eclectics who had two major visions—to terminate colonial rule and to create a modern nation-state. According to Coleman these aspirations were, among other things, bedeviled by cultural differences and the lack of "strong trans-tribal and trans-regional class solidarity" among the new elite.[5] While Coleman correctly explains the process through which national consciousness lost out to ethnonationalism, a more careful and nuanced study should have noted that alienation in some broad sense was neither unique nor special to the political elite—more so under colonial order.

Focusing on changing gender relations, for instance, other studies have argued that the constraints of European patriarchal policy reinforced the preexisting patriarchal structures of traditional Muslim, African societies, with the result that African women were rapidly stripped of their former authority and status.[6] Thus Coleman's view of the elite, as individuals extricated from their culture, stems from a wrong assumption that these individuals had broken their common bonds with the family, kinship and other community-based institutions, whose influences both contributed in shaping and derailing their nationalist visions. Such wrong assumptions also influenced similar studies on the colonial African elite.

By inference, with an intrinsic belief in a glorious African past, the critics of the colonial African intelligentsia had expected the political elite to adopt an attitude to politics that should have ensured pride in indigenous institutions, enthroned peaceful coexistence, and encouraged sustainable development. In fact, their evolutionist view of history was predicated on the belief that, since nationalism had brought progress to the Western world, Africa would likewise achieve development through emphasis on nationalism. In this belief, the critics, on the one hand, expressed optimism of development in line with the West. On the other hand, by approaching colonial studies in a binary vision and in an attempt to assert the love for indigenous institutions, the critics "produced an 'Other,' constructed their own Africa and provided it with an appropriate past."[7]

As crises rocked the ship of the newly independent states, and as the expectations of independence turned into disillusionment, so did the views of African historians on the performance of the emergent African leaders change pessimistically.[8] Wyatt MacGaffey has argued this point with the contention "that the political history of the continent conditions, though it does not determine, the course and content of African studies."[9] One may therefore assert that the allusion to an alienated educated elite proceeded alongside the pessimism of postcolonial leadership. In this context, its adopters refurbished alienation in its Marxist interpretation as a tool to explain African issues. "The distinction between the African and the European, the indigenous and the imported, remained. African leaders were attacked for having betrayed African values for ill-suited Western ones."[10] In retrospect, the critics denounced the political elite's exposure to, and adoption of, Western education, Christian religion, culture, and ideology—all the forces assumed to have contributed to the disruption of African institutions and the supposed elite's alienation.

Among all the writers of the time, E.A. Ayandele was the most critical of the elite. This maverick historian commenced his series of retrospective critiques of the colonial intelligentsia in West Africa in 1971 with a piece on James Africanus B. Horton, a Sierra Leonean recaptive of Igbo parentage. In very strong words, Ayandele described Horton as a de-Africanized being "living in borrowed British milieu of colonial Sierra Leone who knew nothing of the I[g]bo society whose label he claimed."[11] He further claimed that Horton was "un-African," "hypnotized," an "unrepentant Anglophile," "hybridized," and "transmogrified." Persons like Horton represented, Ayandele also argued:

> [A] new species of African—hybridized, transmogrified, and passionate borrowers of Western values, ideas, norms, mores, thought-patterns, religion, and cosmology; deserters of their fatherland's cultural heritage; revellers in the white

> man's mental world; worshippers of white man's
> education; apostles of political, social, and cultural
> aspirations completely at variance with the aspi-
> rations of the rest of the continent.[12]

Pieter Hensbroek, who has made an insightful analysis of Horton and his critics, contends that Horton, the exemplar of modernization discourse in nineteenth century African thought, was ahead of his age. In other words, rather than being discredited or portrayed pejoratively, Horton's "discourse, focusing on Africa's answer to the European challenge," should be appreciated in the Hegelian tradition as an achievement that was uncommon among the wider West African intellectual community of his era.[13] Ayandele's views betray the inherent problem of a binary approach to elite history— hence Hensbroek sees the notion of "alienation" as an unfounded myth. Therefore the perception of Africanus Horton, for instance, "as being alienated from African realities, a 'Black Englishman,'" is seriously flawed on the grounds that such views "do not derive their interpretation from the texts and the specific historical circumstances."[14] As Hensbroek argues, however "sophisticated the historians' ideas and theories may be (which they are often not), such views only develop conjectures about lines of influencing, or advance interest theories, and then ascribe ideas" to subjects they hardly understood. To avoid this error, "the texts themselves, have to be grasped first."[15]

In a sequel, *The Educated Elite*, published in 1975, Ayandele unleashed the most merciless attack on the colonial political intelligentsia. The scope of this attack ran through the succeeding generations of educated African elite. In reference to the earlier generations, Ayandele had maintained that the educated elite were "hybrids in the cultural and sociological sense that whilst they were black in skin, with pure Negro blood, they were superficially and artificially white in their cultural and social ambitions."[16] Ayandele despised the earlier generations for doing little or nothing in condemnation of British colonial rule in Nigeria, including the "verbal pugilists" such as Holy Johnson and Mojola Agbebi who had voiced their resentment to imperial overtures at one point or the other. In Ayandele's view: "the pre-colonial elite were [altogether] a cowardly set of irresponsible deserters of unlettered chiefs and masses when the supreme moment of confrontation came."[17] They were "the vanguards of moral pollution in Nigeria." For Ayandele, their whole personality was psychopathic, "a psychical problem," "lost selves like all Nigerians today inducted in the Western-style education and exposed to the white man's cultural heritage."[18]

As portrayed by Ayandele, the later groups of educated elite were, in many respects, like their predecessors. In his judgment, the modern nationalists, including the so-called radical leaders—Nnamdi Azikiwe, K. O. Mbadiwe, Mazi Mbonu Ojike, and Nwafor Orizu—were all guilty of embracing British imperial rule, having individually "acknowledged the value of British protection."[19] For instance, Mbadiwe not only loved and cherished the British Empire, but also saw "no power on earth to shake the confidence of the West Africans in Great Britain."[20] As late as 1960, R. O. A. Akinjide saw nothing to be "ashamed of Britain being in Nigeria."[21] In 1952 Adegoke Adelabu, widely considered as a cultural nationalist, saw in British colonial rule a favorable development from which Nigeria could fashion a national ethos.[22] Altogether the new men were nothing but "the *beni oui oui*"—a French term meaning "Yes Men" or "His Master's Voice."[23] This is an apt example of what I have characterized here as a historiography of self-damnation.

In an appraisal of Ayandele's study on Nigeria's intelligentsia, Zachernuk asserts the influence of the Nigerian civil war (1967-1970) in his (Ayandele's) passionate illumination of the historical failures of the educated elite, "especially as political leaders, to steer Nigeria away from its postcolonial crises."[24] If Ayandele's judgment of the elite had been informed by his anger over their failures, then his pro-alienation rhetoric must be seen as biased—for it reduces elite history to a discourse of celebration and blame. There is no convincing historical/empirical evidence to support the claim to severance of ties between the elite and their various local communities.

Similar to Ayandele, Zimbabwean scholar David Chanaiwa, in a study on the colonial African political elite in Southern Africa, argues that "Christianity and colonial education have had profoundly disorganizing and divisive effects" by creating two extremes, "the Westernized elite and the traditionalists." According to Chanaiwa, whose views also apply to Nigeria:

> The average modern African nationalist leader was miseducated by the colonizers [and] ended up living in three worlds: the utopian world of universalism, nonracialism, nonviolence, and anti-materialism which they sought to establish here on earth: the practical world of settler colonialism which they misunderstood; and the traditionalist African world which they despised and from which they attempted to escape.[25]

Doing a critique against the background of Africa's unpleasant modern experiences, Chanaiwa argued thus: "the ideas and activities of the colonial-educated elite appear extremely neocolonialist." While recognizing their useful contributions as "the forerunners of modern African cross-ethnic unity, leadership, and Pan-Africanism and as the first leaders to undermine the ethnic, collaborationist potentials of the chiefs," he sees these political elite as politically naïve. Chanaiwa perceives "the goals, structures, and curricula of missionary churches and schools" as primarily meant to create an African population that was "politically acquiescent of

[sic] Christianity and colonial education"—a view zealously shared by others like Moumouni, Rodney and Mazrui.

The aforementioned perception of colonial education as a culturally disruptive force, in Mangan's view, represents "a continuing stereotype" in imperial discourse.[26] Mangan's position subtly draws attention to the subjectivity inherent in the performance appraisal of postcolonial African political leadership: the easy tendency to attribute and discuss leadership failures in postcolonial Africa to the perceived collaborationist and compromising attitude of the emergent leaders to Western values. This stereotype has led to the claim by Chanaiwa and others that the elite "despised African traditionalism and discouraged African historical and racial consciousness."[27] This view, as hinted earlier, reveals an attempt to reduce alienation to a problem of elite/mass gap; while proffering a sort of "back to old Africa" or cultural nationalism as the answer to the continent's postcolonial frustrations.

Afigbo's *Ropes of Sand* represents a good example of this misplaced approach to colonial history.[28] Afigbo took issues with the Eastern Nigerian government under the premiership of Dr. M. I. Okpara (one of the principal Igbo colonial intellectuals) for doing little to protect Igbo culture immediately after independence. As a successor of the colonial government, Afigbo argued that there was no "inspired central direction or leadership"[29] from the government in the promotion of cultural nationalism, especially with regard to the study of the Igbo language.

> Yet one would have expected such action in view of the cultural chauvinism of the nationalist movement. But this could not be. In the first place nationalism emphasized modernization, science education and so on, and that immediately; a programme which placed a high premium on western education and western languages. . . . Here the rather romantic and starry-eyed pan-

Africanist programs of the N.C.N.C. Government which ruled Eastern Nigeria was a handicap
to the flourishing of local cultural nationalism.
[Igbo] rulers dominated by some thorough going
philistines, adopted an ostentatious anti-Igbo
stance without being truly Nigerian.[30]

If clearly understood, Afigbo suggests that the political elite
were a pretentious and self-serving class whose eyes were
completely turned towards Western cultures at the negation
of those indigenous values, which could have made government more meaningful to the people. In this light, Davidson's
more recent study, in its anti-elite stance, attacks the colonial
political elite for their impulse to convert African institutions to European models rather than to conserve them.
He argues that "poverty of speculative thought led Africa's
modern intelligentsia to accept the European nation-state as
appropriate for Africa."[31] Notwithstanding the value of these
views, one must quickly assert their flaws for attempting to
impose a singular or kaleidoscopic world of disparate and
fragmentary continuities.

Overall, one of the most prominent attacks on the leadership failures of the colonial African educated elite remains
The Wretched of the Earth by Frantz Fanon. As a psychiatric
doctor in the service of the French army during the Alge-
rian revolution, Fanon studied the effects of colonialism on
the natives and shared his views on how the attitude of the
African elite was mitigating against the goals of African
regeneration.[32] When Fanon launched his attack on the
African elite for their betrayal of the hopes of independence,
Cooper was right in his masterful conclusion that "the widespread disillusionment with African nation-states in the
present has undoubtedly opened the vision of historians,
intellectuals, and people in a wide variety of situations to
other ways of imagining collectivities."[33]

Fanon's angst and anger against the emergent African elite stemmed partly from what he perceived as their anti-revolutionary approach to decolonization. Although some postcolonial African leaders like Julius Nyerere and Kwame Nkrumah[34] shared the idea of the regeneration of Africa, Fanon asserted that true freedom could only be attained through a violent struggle. In rejection of the African *evolue* culture, Fanon saw the process of decolonization as "always a violent phenomenon."[35] Therefore: "Violent struggle is the only way to become free," united and progressive.[36] For Fanon, independence granted on mutual compromise with the colonialists will result in both national and continent-wide disaster.[37]

The second issue on which Fanon resented the African leaders was also partly based on what he perceived as the lack of a functional ideology among the intellectuals involved in the decolonization rhetoric. Fanon considered a people-centered ideology (a threshold of socialism), as a means to "give the continent a framework for unity and create a feeling of common purpose and solidarity among the different peoples and states."[38]

Fanon's thought was constructed from a view of colonial Africa as a "Manichean world" in which the colonizer and colonized were at extreme opposites with no intermediary. For Fanon, colonial racism was a class issue.[39] The resulting effect of the polar opposition of evil and good, white and black, rich and poor, exploiter and exploited, was the culmination of the need for Africans to violently bring about regeneration.[40] As Hensbroek underscored, in Fanon's concept of colonial alienation, "The personality is the exemplar for the political; political liberation is a therapeutic process, a process of reestablishing collective identity."[41] Therefore the issue of liberation involved overcoming psychological alienation, hence at the individual level violence was encouraged as a healing balm. "It frees the native from his inferiority complex and from his despair and inaction; it makes him fearless and restores his self-respect."[42]

Hensbroek's critical evaluation of Fanon reveals a number of weaknesses in his thinking. For example, Fanon's mythical concept "of a pregiven nation" ("the people or the oppressed") that was subsequently alienated under colonial domination is questioned as being both historically and theoretically erroneous. The error stems from the perception of the "rich and diverse heritages of peoples, life forms, religions, and cultures" as a single entity.[43] Yet, the fundamental problem remains that Fanon's attack on the elite was politically motivated. He wrongly assumed that violence and people-centered ideology, as he advocated, were automatic answers to the complexities of Africa's regeneration—an agenda some African leaders patriotically labored to achieve.

Summary and Concluding Comments

This response, based on the theme of Professor Waibinte Wariboko's inaugural address, focused on the intersection between European Christian missionary activities and the invention of a derogatory African identity and personhood over the period of colonial rule. This development explains the rise of a peculiar form of nationalist historiography that used and abused evidence in its quest for a useable past to inform Africa's postcolonial development. To explain this problem in African history, I have used the example of the mainstream views of the colonial African elite. The evidence reveals that the notion of an alienated generation of African educated elite, and mostly the immediate post-colonial leaders, was premised on an attempt to hold these people squarely responsible for Africa's postcolonial problems. Coleman, Ayandele, Chanaiwa, Afigbo, Fanon, and others, share a common view that the poor performances of these leaders had to do with their exposure and wholesome acceptance of Western influences. This brutal assessment of African nationalists and the immediate postcolonial leaders, however, would have been different if the postcolonial state in Africa had maintained a steady developmental progress. No doubt, Western influences would have been viewed from a different perspective also. The point here is that, so far as development crises, rather than empirical/historical facts, form the core premise on which the elite are dismissed as alienated individuals, this judgment cannot be anything but biased. Pro-alienation discourse, in order to go beyond its damning critique of the postcolonial elite, has to undertake a more comprehensive assessment of the many and varied factors hindering development of the African postcolonial state.

Overall, it is important that historians should not err in the direction of social scientists who are more concerned with failures of the present than with the more pertinent questions about how we arrived at the present situation. The historiography of self-assertion must not be misused or else we lose our moral superiority and fall flat on similar abuses brought about by prideful and desperate aliens totting a false brand of Christianity predicated on materialism.

Notes

1. See: C. J. Korieh and R. C. Njoku, *Missions, States, and European Expansion in Africa* (New York and London: Routledge, 2007).

2. W.E. Wariboko, *Ruined by Race: Afro-Caribbean Missionaries and the Evangelization of Southern Nigeria, 1895-1925* (Trenton, NJ: African World Press, 2006).

3. J.S. Coleman, *Nigeria: Background to Nationalism* (Berkeley and Los Angeles: University of California Press, 1958).

4. In retrospect, Coleman (*Nigeria*, 161) argued that the tempo and course of nationalism in Nigeria might have been dif-

ferent had the British authorities avoided the dualism of excluding educated Africans on grounds of principle, but at the same time giving them the vision of ultimate control.

5. Coleman, *Nigeria*, 409-15. For similar views see: E. A. Ayandele, *The Missionary Impact on Modern Nigeria 1842-1914: A Political and Social Analysis* (London: Longman, 1966), see Chapter 8, 241-50; P. S. Zachernuk, *Colonial Subjects: An African Intelligentsia and Atlantic Ideas.* Charlottesville, Virginia: University Press of Virginia, 2000) 124; F. Fanon, *The Wretched of the Earth* - preface by Jean-Paul Satire, translation by Constance Farrington- (New York: Grove Press, 1963); R. L. Sklar, *Nigerian Political Parties: Power in an Emergent African Nation* (Princeton, New Jersey: Princeton University Press, 1963); Billy Dudley; *An Introduction to Nigerian Government and Politics* (Bloomington: Indiana University Press, 1982).

6. See: N. Mba, *Women's Political Activity in Southern Nigeria, 1900-1965* (Berkeley: University of California Institute for International Studies, 1982) 38. Mba's study illustrates how the colonial system rendered women "invincible to the exclusively male colonial administrators," notwithstanding the small gains for women under the new legal system in matters of marriage and divorce, as well as authority in the indigenous churches (67). See also J. L. Parpart, *Women and the State in Africa* (Michigan: Michigan State University, 1986) 7-8; L. Denzer, "Gender and Decolonization: A Study of Three Women in West African Public Life," in *People and Empires in African History: Essays in Memory of Michael Crowder.* eds. J.F.A. Ajayi and J.D.Y. Peel. (London: Longman, 1992) 217-36.

7. B. Jewsiewicki, "Introduction: One Historiography or Several?" in *African Historiographies: What History for which Africa?* eds. B. Jewsiewicki & D. Newbury. (Beverly Hills: Sage Publications, 1986) 10-11; see also A.L. Stoler and F. Cooper, "Between Metropole and Colony: Rethinking a Research Agenda" in *Tensions of Empire: Colonial Cultures in a Bourgeois World* eds. A.L. Stoler and F. Cooper. (Berkeley, California: University of California Press, 1997), 5. The

authors have observed that "the flood of recent scholarship have located in the colonies the 'Other' against whom the very idea of Europeanness was expressed." For details, see related studies like E. Said, *Orientalism* (New York: Pantheon Books, 1978); T. Todorov, *On Human Diversity: Nationalism, Racism, and Exoticism in French Thought* (Cambridge: Harvard University Press, 1993); A. Behdad, *Belated Travelers: Orientalism in the Age of Colonial Desolation* (Durham: Duke University Press, 1994).

8. See A. J. Temu and B. Swai, *Historians and Africanist History, a Critique: Post-colonial Historiography Examined* (London: Westport, Conn.: Zed Press, 1981), 19, 63. According to the authors, soon, the "high noon of postcolonial African historiography" was over, as the "golden age of consensus" among writers changed. See also D.B. Abernethy, *The Political Dilemma of Popular Education: An African Case* (California: Stanford University Press, 1969), 10. In his later writings on political decay and breakdown of modernization among Afro-Asian states, Abernethy offered a counterbalance to the optimistic descriptions of the early 1960s.

9. W. MacGaffey, "Epistemological Ethnocentrism in African Studies," in *African Historiographies*, eds. Jewsiewicki and Newbury. 47.

10. Zachernuk, *Subjects*, 3.

11. E. A. Ayandele, "James Africanus Beale Horton, 1835-1883: Prophet of Modernization in West Africa," *African Historical Studies* 4, no. 3 (1971): 696. This article was a review on Horton's *West African Countries and Peoples,* with an introduction by George Shepperson (1868; reprint Chicago: Aldine Publishers Company, 1969).

12. Ayandele, "Horton," 691. Ayandele claimed that the educated elite "had more in common with the whites in Europe and America, than with the multimillion unlettered Africans in the vast interior of the continent." See also: P. B. V. Hensbroek, *Political Discourse in African Thought 1860 to the Present* (Westport, CT: Praeger Publishers, 1999), 38.

13. Hensbroek, *Discourse,* 25. For a more positive view of Horton, see A.O. Nwauwa, "Far Ahead of his Time: James Africanus Horton's Initiatives for a West African University and his Frustrations, 1862-1871," *Cahiers d' etudes africaines* 153, nos. 39-1 (1999) 107-21.

14. Hensbroek, *Discourses,* 39.

15. Hensbroek, *Discourses,* 39.

16. E.A. Ayandele, *The Educated Elite in the Nigerian Society: University Lecture* (Ibadan, Nigeria: Ibadan University Press, 1974) 28.

17. Ayandele, *Educated Elite,* 56, 57-8. According to the author, by 1910, all the educated elite had accepted the establishment of British colonial rule, including the few cultural nationalists like James Johnson and Mojola Agbebi. There was no question of their organizing protests against the colonialists. Potts-Johnson equally may fall within this group of collaborators. According to Dixon-Fyle, "The Potts-Johnson of this period was no radical nationalist, seeking an end to British control of Port Harcourt. Like Zik and others, he sought a period of political tutelage, which would get the Africans ready for self-government. Otherwise, to demand self-government without preparation would amount to "putting the cart before the horse." See M. Dixon-Fyle, *A Saro Community in the Niger Delta, 1912-1984: the Potts-Johnsons of Port Harcourt and their Heirs* (Rochester, NY: University of Rochester Press, 1999) 60.

18. Ayandele, *Educated Elite,* 28-42. As a point of observation, Dixon-Fyle, at least, indicates an exception to Ayandele's rather sweeping generalization on individualism. This exception was L.R. Potts-Johnson, who in a spirit of "cooperation and self-help" admonished his peers to discontinue to "live in our congenial atmosphere of individualism." See Dixon-Fyle, *Saro,* 38.

19. Ayandele, *Educated Elite,* 59. For a strong critic of Ayandele's thesis, see P.O. Esedebe, "The Educated Elite in Nigeria Reconsidered," *JHSN* 10, no. 3 (1980): 111-30.

20. K. O. Mbadiwe, *British and Axis Aim in Africa* (New York: Wendell Malliet, 1942) 164, 242.

21. R.O.A. Akinjide cited in Ayandele, *Educated Elite*, 59.

22. A. Adelabu, *Africa in Ebullition* (Ibadan: the author, 1952) 28; See Ayandele, *Educated Elite*, 60.

23. Ayandele, *Educated Elite*, 70. Ayandele emphasized that for the educated elite, including "the so-called nationalists," loyalty for the British Crown was "an article of faith" (73).

24. Zachernuk, *Subjects*, 5. This observation is correct in view of the fact that the pieces on Horton and the educated elite in Nigeria were produced at the end of the civil war (1967-70).

25. D. Chanaiwa, "Colonial Education in Southern Africa," in *Independence Without Freedom: The Political Economy of Colonial Education in Southern Africa* eds. A. Mugomba and M. Nyaggah (Santa Barbara: ABC-CLIO, 1980), 221. See also: A. Mazrui, *Political Values and the Educated Class in Africa* (Berkeley, California: University of California Press, 1978).

26. Chanaiwa, "Colonial Education," 222; A. Moumouni, *Education in Africa* (New York: Frederick A. Praeger Publishers, 1968) 50-3; W. Rodney, *How Europe Underdeveloped Africa* (London: Bogle-L'Ouverture Publications, 1972), 261-86; Mazrui, *Political Values*. See also: J. A. Mangan, "Images for Confident Control: Stereotypes in Imperial Discourses," in *The Imperial Curriculum: Racial Images and Education in British Colonial Experience*. ed. J.A. Mangan. (London and New York: Routledge, 1993), 6-21.

27. Chanaiwa, "Colonial Education," 221-2. In the opinion of Chanaiwa, the real historical relevance of the colonial African intellectuals is mostly seen in their "their commitment to high intellectual standards." Otherwise, in his judgment, they contrast with the succeeding African nationalists who had to abandon the "reformist, capitalist" strategies of the older political elite for a militant struggle against those Western interests and values that have the tendency to destroy the dignity of the African. See also Basil Davidson, *The Black*

Man's Burden: Africa and the Curse of the Nation-State (New York: Times Books, 1992) 229-31, 42.

28. A.E. Afigbo, *The Warrant Chiefs: Indirect Rule in Southern Nigeria* (London: Longman, 1972); and *Ropes of Sand: Studies in Igbo History and Culture* (Nsukka and Oxford: University Press, 1981).

29. Afigbo, *Ropes*, 384.

30. Ibid.

31. Davidson, *Burden*, 49-50; also see also Zachernuk, *Subjects*, 5. The latter has criticized this approach of study as more of a condemnatory exercise than exploratory..

32. See Fanon, *Wretched;* see also A.K. Armah, "African Socialism: Utopia or Scientific?" *Presence Africaine* 64 (1967) 6-30; R.H. Chilcote, *Amilcar Cabral's Revolutionary Theory and Practice: A Critical Guide* (Boulder, Colorado: L. Rienner Publishers, 1991); P. Chabal, *Amilcar Cabral: Revolutionary Leadership and People's War* (Cambridge and New York: Cambridge University Press, 1983); Davidson, *Burden* (1992); Ayandele, *Missionary;* "The Nigerian Elite," in *Nigerian Historical Studies* (London: Frank Cass, 1979).

33. Cooper, "Africa's Pasts," 326.

34. See Kwame Nkrumah, *Consciencism: Philosophy and Ideology for Decolonization and Development with Particular Reference to the African Revolution* (London: Toronto: Heinemann, 1964); *Towards Colonial Freedom: Africa in the Struggle against World Imperialism* (London, Heinemann, 1962); Julius Nyerere, *Freedom and Socialism. Uhuru na Ujamaa: A Selection from Writings and Speeches, 1965-1967* (Dar es Salaam, New York: Oxford University Press, 1968).

35. Fanon, *Wretched*, 36-7.

36. Hensbroek, *Discourses*, 120.

37. E. Obiechina, "Frantz Fanon: The Man and His Works," *Ufahamu* 3 (1972) 114.

38. Obiechina, "Frantz Fanon," 108.

39. R. Zahar, *Frantz Fanon: Colonialism and Alienation* - translation by Willfried F. Feuser - (New York and London: Monthly Review Press, 1974) 18-26.

40. Fanon, *Wretched,* 41. In this compartment, according to Fanon, the native is declared insensible to ethics. Mazrui in *Political Values*, 25, provides an insightful explanation on "Manicheans": an ancient religious order that can help deepen insight on the context in which Fanon used the term in his description of the colonial order. The sect, which existed during the time of St. Augustine, claimed that there were two guiding principles on earth. One they called *Ormuzed*, the principle of Light, of Goodness, and of God. The opposite, *Ahriman*, was the principle of Darkness or Satan. Thus, the virtuous, as held by the sect, "was the man who had as little dealings as possible with *Ahriman*.".

41. Hensbroek, *Discourses,* 121.

42. Fanon, *Wretched,* 94.

43. Hensbroek, *Discourses,* 122

SELECT BIBLIOGRAPHY

Alagoa, E.J. *The Practice of History in Africa*. Port Harcourt: Onyoma Research Publications, 2007.

————. *The Python's Eye: The Past in the Living Present* Port Harcourt: Harrison Publication Company 1977 (University of Port Harcourt Inaugural Lecture).

Austen, A.R. and Smith, W.D. "Images of Africa and British Slave Trade Abolition: The Transition to an Imperialist Ideology, 1787-1807," *African Historical Studies* 2, no. 1 (1969).

Armstrong, R.G. *The Study of West African Languages*. Ibadan: Ibadan University Press, 1967.

Afigbo, A.E. *The Poverty of African Historiography*. Lagos: Afrografika Publishers, 1977.

Appiah, K.A. *In My Father's House: Africa in the Philosophy of Culture*. Oxford: Oxford University Press, 1992.

————. "Identity, Authenticity, Survival: Multicultural Societies and Social Reproduction," in *Multiculturalism*. ed. C. Taylor. Princeton, NJ: Princeton University Press, 1964.

————. "Race, Culture, and Identity: Misunderstood Connections," in *Colour Consciousness: The Political Morality of Race*. ed. K.A. Appiah and A. Gutman. Princeton, NJ: Princeton University Press, 1996.

Abernethy, D.B. *The Political Dilemma of Popular Education: An African Case* California: Stanford Univ. Press, 1969.

Akbar, N. *Breaking the Chains of Psychological Slavery* Tallahassee, FL: Mind Productions & Associates, 1996 .

Ayandele, E.A. "James Africanus Beale Horton, 1835-1883: Prophet of Modernization in West Africa" *African Historical Studies* 4, No. 3 (1971).

_____. *The Educated Elite in the Nigerian Society: University Lecture* Ibadan: Nigeria: Ibadan Univ. Press 1974.

Basden, G.T. *Among the Ibos of Nigeria.* London: Frankcass 1921. Reprint, London: Frankcass, 1966.

Biko, S.B. "Black Consciousness and the Quest for True Humanity," in *The African Philosophical Reader*. ed. P.H. Coetzee and A.P.J. Roux. London: Routledge, 2003.

Bersselaar, P.H. "Missionary Knowledge and the State in Colonial Nigeria: On How G.T. Basden Became an Expert" *History of Africa* 33 (2006).

Baron, J.T. "James Stephen, the 'Black Race' and British Colonial Administration, 1813-47" *Journal of Imperial and Commonwealth History* V, no. 2 (January 1977).

Barkan, E. *The Retreat of Scientific Racism.* Cambridge: Cambridge University Press, 1992.

Bersselaar, V.D. D. *The King of Drinks: Schnapps Gin from Modernity to Tradition* Leiden: Brill, 2007 .

Bessis, B. *Western Supremacy: The Triumph of an Idea?* New York: Zed Books, 2001.

Ballantyne, T. "Empire, Knowledge and Culture: From Proto-Globalization to Modern Globalization" in *Globalization in World History*. ed. A.G. Hopkins. London: Pimilco, 2002.

Cohn, B. *Colonialism and its Forms of Knowledge: The British in India* Princeton: Princeton Univ. Press, 1996.

Cooper, F. & Brubaker, "Identity" in *Colonialism in Question: Theory, Knowledge, History*. ed. F. Cooper. Berkeley and Los Angeles: Univ. of California Press, 2005 .

Curtin, P.D. *The Image of Africa. 1780-1850* Madison: The University of Wisconsin Press, 1964.

_____."'Scientific' Racism and British Theory of Empire," *Journal of the Historical Society of Nigeria*, 2, no1 (1960) .

Coombes, A. *Reinventing Africa: Museums, Material Culture and Popular Imagination* New Haven: Yale Univ. Press, 1994.

Collingwood, R.G. *The Idea of History*. London: Clarendon Press 1946. Reprint, Oxford: Oxford: University Press, 1978.

Conway, A. *The History of the Negro in the United States* London: The Historical Association, London, 1968.

Deegan, H. *The Politics of the New South Africa: Apartheid and After*. New York: Longman, 2001.

Eze, E.C. *Race and the Enlightenment*. Oxford: Blackwell, 1997.

Falola, T. *Nationalism and African Intellectuals* Rochester: Univ. of Rochester Press 2001.

Fraser, D. *The Future of Africa*, London: Young Peoples Missionary Movement 1911. Reprint, Westport, CT: Negro University Press. 1970.

Fields, B. "Slavery, Race and Ideology in the United States of America" *New Left Review* 181 (1990).

Freire, P. *The Pedagogy of the Oppressed*, Penguin: England. 1990.

Fanon, F. *The Wretched of the Earth* New York: Grove Press, 1963.

Gordon, L.R. *Disciplinary Decadence: Living Thought in Trying Times*. London: Paradigm Publishers, 2006.

Gilroy, P. *Against Race: Imagining Political Culture beyond the Color Line*. Cambridge: Cambridge University Press, 2000.

Hampton, H. and Fayer, S. *Voices of Freedom: An Oral History of the Civil Rights Movement from the 1950s through the 1980s* New York: Bantam Books, 1990.

Hayward, R.J. "AfroAsiatic" in *African Languages: An Introduction*. ed. B. Heine and D. Nurse. Cambridge University Press, 2000.

Hegel, G.W.F. *The Philosophy of History*. New York: Dover Publications, 1956.

Jordon, W.D. *The White Man's Burden: Historical Origins of Racism in the United States*. Oxford: Oxford University Press, 1974.

Kenyatta, J. *Facing Mount Kenya*. London: Heineman, 1979.

Kirby, J.P. "Cultural Change and Religious Conversion in West Africa" in *Religions in Africa*. eds. D.T. Blakely, E.A.W. Beek, & D.L. Thomson. London: Heinemann, 1994.

Law, R. "The 'Hamitic Hypothesis' in Indigenous West African Historical Thought" *History in Africa* 36 (2009).

Mills, C.W. *The Racial Contract*. Ithaca, NY: Cornell University Press, 1997.

_____. *Blackness Visible: Essays on Philosophy and Race*. London: Cornell University Press, 1998.

Midgley, C. "Anti-Slavery and the Roots of 'Imperial Feminism'" in *Gender and Imperialism*. ed. C. Midgley. Manchester: Manchester Univ. Press, 1998 .

Malik, K. *The Meaning of Race: Race, History and Culture in Western Society*. London: MacMillan Press, 1996.

Mkandawire, T. ed. *African Intellectuals: Rethinking Politics, Language, and Development*. London: Zed Books, 2005.

Meredith, M. *The State of Africa: A History of Fifty Years of Independence*. London: Free Press, 2005.

Mbiti, J.S. *African Religions and Philosophy*. Oxford: Heinemann, 1989.

Mudimbe, V.Y. *The Invention of Africa: Gnosis, Philosophy, and the Order of Knowledge* London: James Currey, 1988.

Mangan, J.A. "Images for Confident Control: Stereotypes in Imperial Discourses" in *The Imperial Curriculum: Racial Images and Education in British Colonial Experience* ed. Mangan, J.A. London and New York: Routledge, 1993.

Nettleford, R.M. *Mirror Mirror: Identity, Race and Protest in Jamaica*. Kingston: LMH Printing Limited, 1998.

Ngugi, J. "The Independence of Africa and Cultural Decolonization" *UNESCO Courier* 1972. Reprint, *Vox Africana* nos. 7,8& 9 (1972).

Newton, A.P. "Africa and Historical Research" *Journal of the African Society* 22, 1922-3.

Ochwada, H. "Historians, Nationalism and Pan-Africanism: Myths and Realities" in *African Intellectual: Rethinking Politics, Language, Gender and Development*. ed. T. Mkandawire. New York: Zed Books, 2005.

Palmer, G.H. *The Enlightenment Abolished: Citizens of Britishness*. Midlothian-Scotland: Henry Publishers, 2007.

Paden, J.N. & Soja, E.W. eds. *The African Experience Volume One: Essays* Evanston: Northwestern University Press 1970 .

Ranger, T. "The Invention of Tradition in Colonial Africa" in *Perspectives on Africa*. ed. R.R. Grinker and C.B. Steiner. Oxford: Blackwell, 1997 .

Rugemer, E.B. *The Problem of Emancipation: The Caribbean Roots of the American Civil War* Baton Rouge: Louisiana State Univ. Press 2008.

Stoler, A.L. & Cooper, F. eds. *Tensions of Empire: Colonial Cultures in a Bourgeois World* Berkeley, California: Univ. of California Press, 1997 .

Said, E. *Orientalism* New York: Pantheon Books, 1978.

Shack, W.A. & Skinner E.P. eds. *Strangers in African Societies*. Berkeley: University of California Press, 1979.

Sanders, E.R. "The Hamitic Hypothesis: Its Origins and Functions in Time Perspective" *Journal of African History* Vol. 10, no.4, (1969).

Shelby, T. *We who are Dark: The Philosophical Foundations of Black Solidarity*. Cambridge-Massachusetts: The Belknap Press of the Harvard University Press, 2005.

Schreuder, D.M. "The Cultural Factor in Victorian Imperialism" *Journal of Imperial and Commonwealth History*, IV, no. 3 (May 1976).

Sherlock, P. *Jamaica's Proud Heritage* (Undated monograph published by the Office of the Vice Chancellor, Mona Campus, The University of the West Indies; and endorsed by the National Council on Education, Jamaica).

Seligman, C.G. *Races of Africa*. London: Home University Library, 1930. Reprint, Oxford: Oxford University Press, 1979.

Thomas, N. *Colonialism's Culture: Anthropology, Travel and Government* Cambridge: Polity Press, 1994 .

Trevor-Roper, H. "The Rise of Christian Europe" *The Listener* 28 November 1963.

Thomas, K. "Ain't Nothin Like the Real Thing: Black Masculinity, Gay Sexuality, and the Jargon of Authenticity" in *The House that Race Built*. ed. W. Lubiano. New York: Vintage Books, 1998.

Tasie, G.O.M. *Christian Missionary Enterprise in the Niger Delta, 1864-1918*. Leiden: E.J. Brill, 1978.

Temu, A.J. & Swai, B. *Historians and Africanist History, a Critique: Post-Colonial Historiography Examined* London: Westport, Connecticut: Zed Press, 1981.

Todorov, T. *On Human Diversity: Nationalism, Racism, and Exoticism in French Thought* Cambridge: Harvard University Press, 1993.

Williams, J.J. *Hebrewisms of West Africa*. New York: The Dial Press, 1930.

Wariboko, W.E. *Planting Church Culture in New Calabar: Some Neglected Aspects of Missionary Enterprise in the Eastern Niger Delta, 1865-1918*. Bethesda-MD: International Scholars Publications, 1998.

_____. "West Indian Church in West Africa: The Pongas Mission among the Susus and its Portrayal of Blackness, 1851-1935" in *Missions, States, and European Expansion in Africa*. ed. Korieh, C.J. and Njoku, R.C. New York: Routledge, 2007.

_____. "James Norris Cheetham and the CMS Civilizing Mission to Igboland: An examination of His Letters to the *Southport Visitor*, 1899- 1931" *The Nigerian Academic Forum* Vol. 6, no. 3 (April 2004).

_____. *Ruined by 'Race': Afro-Caribbean Missionaries and the Evangelization of Southern Nigeria, 1895-1925*. Trenton, NJ: Africa World Press, 2007.

Williams, C. *The Destruction of Black Civilizations: Great Issues of a Race from 4500 BC to 2000 AD.* Chicago-Illinois: Third World Press, 1987 .

West, R.W. *Brazza of the Congo: Exploration and Exploitation in Equatorial Africa.* London: Redwood Press, 1973.

West, C. *Race Matters.* Boston: Beacon, 1993.

Wolfers, M. *Black Man's Burden Revisited.* London: Allison& Busby Limited, 1974.

Zachernuk, P.S. *Colonial Subjects: An African Intelligentsia and Atlantic Ideas* Charlottesville, Virginia: Univ. Press of Virginia, 2000.

Zahar, R. *Frantz Fanon: Colonialism and Alienation* (translation by Willfried F. Feuser) New York and London: Monthly Review Press, 1974.